Teleworking Mum

The essential

Work from Home Guide

for parents

Maria Montesano

Published by Red Bullet Research and Communications, Melbourne, Australia.

Copyright © 2010 Montesano, Maria. All rights reserved.

No part of this publication may be reproduced, stored in a retrieval system or transmitted in any form by any means without prior permission from the author or publisher.

Disclaimer

Every effort has been made to ensure this book is free from error or omissions. The names of persons in this book have been changed to protect the individuals' privacy. The information in this book is of a general nature and does not intend to be advice, nor does it justify readers to act on this information without obtaining professional advice from a taxation advisor, accountant or financial planner. The publisher and author disclaim all and any liability to all and any person, whether they have purchased this book or not, if they have done or omitted to be done, or relied upon the whole or any part of this book. The publisher and author shall not be liable for any loss of profit or any other commercial or personal damages, including but not limited to special, incidental, consequential, or other damages.

Cataloguing-in-Publication (CiP)

Author:	Montesano, Maria
Title:	Teleworking mum : the essential work from home guide for parents / Maria Montesano
Publisher:	Melbourne: Red Bullet Research and Communications, 2010
ISBN:	978-0-9808516-0-1 (pbk.)
ISBN:	978-0-9808516-1-8 (eBook)
Subjects:	1. Telecommuting 2. Home-based businesses 3. Self-employed women--Management 4. Self-employed--Management
Dewey Number:	331.2568

www.teleworkingmum.com.au

TABLE OF CONTENTS

PREFACE 5

INTRODUCTION 7

CHAPTER 1   SMARTER WORK CHOICES FOR MUMS 9

CHAPTER 2   TELEWORKING FACTS 21

CHAPTER 3   FINANCIAL BENEFITS 39

CHAPTER 4   RETURNING TO WORK 55

CHAPTER 5   THE 'F' WORD (FLEXIBILITY) 83

CHAPTER 6   IS IT RIGHT FOR YOU? 95

CHAPTER 7   TELEWORK OPPORTUNITIES 107

CHAPTER 8   TELEWORK ACTION PLAN 121

CHAPTER 9   FAMILY FRIENDLY WORKPLACES 147

CHAPTER 10   WORK AT HOME ESSENTIALS 155

CHAPTER 11   STARTING A HOME-BASED BUSINESS 171

CHAPTER 12   TELEWORKING MUM'S TIMELINE 185

CHAPTER 13   YOUR JOURNEY BEGINS 193

INDEX 198

REFERENCES 199

ABOUT THE AUTHOR 200

Preface

Although I didn't realise it at the time, I started teleworking back in the early 1990's when I landed my first job as a Research Assistant for Deakin University. My department was based in the historic Stonnington building in Toorak where I worked from, initially, until one of the language professors returned from her overseas trip and reclaimed her office space. Rather than waste precious time waiting for a desk and computer to become available I took my work home, and it all started from there.

I found myself working far more productively at home; I was in a more comfortable environment, I was more organised and thrived in my new found autonomy. My employer was impressed with my progress and extended my six month assignment to several years.

My career later moved into the commercial arena where I became quickly absorbed in the typical corporate culture: long commutes in peak hour traffic, working ten to twelve hour days and taking work home every weekend. I was completely exhausted.

In anticipation of one day starting a family, I realised that the corporate office was not the place for me – well, not as a mum, anyway. So, I began looking at less demanding work roles as a solution to being able to juggle the two aspects of my life with more ease and satisfaction. I resigned from my role which had taken me two tertiary qualifications and thirteen years of experience to get to, and started my own small business in retail.

Like most small business owners, I managed everything on my own: sales, marketing, advertising, bookkeeping, accounting, stock control, merchandising, web design and cleaning. Eventually I hired casual staff to assist me. My plan was to hire a manager several months into my pregnancy to take over my position whilst I took time off from the business to focus on bringing my first child into the world. However, things didn't quite go as planned.

From the moment I became pregnant I was struck with a continuous stream of health issues. The severity of illnesses inhibited me from sourcing and training someone to replace me. I therefore relied on my junior staff to keep the business afloat whilst I was bed ridden at home or in hospital. With my chronic absence and lack of direction, not surprisingly, the business went downhill quickly.

With no maternity leave options and desperate to save my business, I found myself back at work less than three weeks after the birth of my newborn son. I was physically and mentally depleted. Emotionally I was a nervous wreck, as I found myself fighting a huge emotional battle every time I had to go to work. The problem was simply that I did not want to leave my newborn baby in someone else's care. Furthermore, I was not physically well enough to deal with the demands of work in conjunction with the sleep deprivation that ensued after childbirth.

As a result, I closed my business to stay home to tend to my responsibilities as a mother and also allow myself time to heal after the difficulties experienced during pregnancy and childbirth.

The dilemma I then faced, however, was that my contribution to the family's income was a necessity. At that point, plagued with so many obstacles, I exhausted every avenue I could fathom as a solution to my predicament. The only glimmer of hope I found was to pursue the possibility of working from home.

෨෬

I am now a Teleworking Mum, and have been since my pledge almost five years ago. I must admit, most people are surprised - even shocked - to hear that I work. They see me at home every day, taking care of my baby and my pre-school aged son and assume I'm a regular *'stay at home mum'*. What most people don't realise is that I also earn a living at home utilising my skills as a researcher.

Everyone who initially learns of my teleworking arrangement always inundates me with questions about how I came across this brilliant opportunity: a great employer, a decent pay and the flexibility and support to work from home. Most people think this sounds too good to be true, but it's not - it's my reality.

This has been the source of my inspiration for creating this book. I wanted to help other mums understand that life doesn't need to be a struggle, a fight or a huge sacrifice because you want or need to return to work. I want to encourage other mothers to take that leap of faith and trust that there is a better way to live and work in harmony.

Introduction

The journey towards creating this book started early in 2008. At that time the world economy was in turmoil and, as a direct result, many pressing issues were affecting families all around the world. Some of these included soaring petrol prices, rising mortgage interest rates and the high cost of living. During the latter part of 2008 Europe declared it was in a recession and the US feared the greatest depression of all. Australia was bracing for a similar fate.

Research has shown that telework (i.e., working from home) stimulates the economy in many ways, including sustaining employment levels. By delivering significant financial benefits it enables businesses to retain staff, increase productivity levels by up to forty percent and considerably improve business efficiencies.

With such extensive business incentives, it is no surprise that teleworking is now becoming an intrinsic business strategy, rather than just a way of working. For employees, telework is becoming the work-style choice of the future, enabling them to integrate their family, work and personal lives more harmoniously. For businesses, telework could potentially make the difference between survival and failure (particularly during a period of economic vulnerability).

The information in this book is applicable in any economic climate; however, during a downturn or even recession, it amplifies the benefits with a clear objective to achieve a win win for both employees and employers. In fact when you read the chapter on the far-reaching benefits that telework offers, you might say it offers a win, win, win, win opportunity (benefiting employees, employers, the community and the economy).

Whilst the general principles of this book can be applied by anyone wishing to work from home, it is aimed largely at mothers of dependent children. Of course this also includes fathers, adoptive parents and other carers with a primary care responsibility for children. It could also be aptly applied to carers of ill, elderly or disabled persons.

Lately, the topic of mums and work has become a regular feature throughout the media and is also attracting significant political focus.

This is largely driven by the urgent need to address the glaring disconnection between the work/life fit of mothers.

Traditionally, mothers have been the main providers of care for children and their role was predominantly confined within the private domain (i.e., the home). In recent times, mums have progressively moved into the public domain (i.e., the workforce), yet their role as primary carer also remains intact. This dual work/life role creates a significant conflict for mums, creating a collision of time, commitments and priorities.

The fact that more women are nowadays having children later in life means that there is an increasing trend for them to be enduring a double caring responsibility – that of child and elderly or ill parents. This places further pressure on women, depriving them of time and limiting their ability to pursue vocational aspirations, or indeed, simply earning a living. There are a significant number of women who drop out of the workforce as they derive no worthwhile benefits from returning to work, when there are limited or no flexible work choices open to them.

Teleworking, a leading flexible work style, reduces many of the barriers that impede workforce participation or re-entry for mums. The Australian government has formally acknowledged the significant impact that flexible working arrangements can make to the country's economic and social wellbeing, by endorsing such workforce practices through the introduction of the Fair Work Act 2009. As of 1st January, 2010, eligible workers with a primary care responsibility, now have the right to request flexible working arrangements from their employer. Telework (i.e., working from home) is a fundamental flexible work style. If you've ever wanted to work from home, or have been longing for a better way to manage your work/life demands, there's no better time than now to harness the many benefits that teleworking offers.

Chapter 1

Smarter Work Choices for Mums

Breaking down the barriers

Motherhood changes your entire universe. It seems everything is suddenly transformed to accommodate your newfound family. This major shift in life often affects the way in which many women perceive their jobs or careers. What was once a keen focus might now be seen as a major obstacle, or even an interference.[1]

The transition from motherhood to workforce re-entry is a very complex and often difficult one. It's commonly fraught with physical, emotional, financial and logistical issues, just to name a few! Teleworking (meaning working from home using some form of technology or communications) offers a smarter, more fulfilling journey for mums wanting – or needing – to return to work. It helps break down some of the barriers that often stand

---

[1] Pocock et al, AWALI, 2009, discusses the notion of 'work/life interference' as being a more realistic depiction of experience for working mothers, as opposed to 'work/life balance'.

in the way from making workforce re-entry viable or even possible. Typical dilemmas faced by mums re-entering the workforce include:

- Lack of time
- High childcare costs
- Unavailability of suitable or preferred childcare
- Emotional / separation issues
- Physical and health issues
- Breastfeeding routines
- Conflicting work/family demands
- High work-related costs (e.g., commute or parking fees, wardrobe expenses)
- Logistical issues (e.g., drop-off and pick-up times for school or childcare)

Not surprisingly, one in five mothers opts out of the workforce altogether, many of whom are unable to resolve these pressing issues. Telework is a powerful work style choice for mums because it can potentially reduce or eliminate these problems.

The 'F' word (i.e., 'flexibility') is a vital ingredient for making workforce participation viable for mums. Teleworking is a prominent flexible work style which enables an easier, faster and less stressful return to work avenue than the traditional employer-based job. Particularly when used in conjunction with other flexible working arrangements, such as part-time hours, flextime, job share, etc., teleworking can make a profound difference to the quality of life for mums and their families.

Australia has recently introduced new legislation supporting workplace flexibility. Eligible mothers (or primary carers) of young children now have the 'right to request' suitable flexible working arrangements from their employer. Chapter 5 explains these new laws, outlining your rights and your employer's legal obligations in relation to your request.

All about the money

Research indicates that most mums return to work for financial reasons. However, the problem faced by many mums returning to a traditional job, at their employer's location, is that they often find that any financial gains expected from earning an income are either markedly reduced or completely ruled out when childcare and other work costs come into the equation. (Think of what it would cost you to pay for childcare, commute/parking fees, wardrobe costs, lunches, grooming, etc.)

Teleworking considerably reduces – or even removes - many work-related costs. This is usually achieved through the reduction or elimination of commuting, childcare, corporate wardrobe and other expenses.

What many people don't realise is that teleworking also provides many hidden financial benefits. For example, teleworking potentially enables you to:
- Claim back many household-related expenses such as utility bills, telephone bills, internet subscriptions, and possibly even mortgage interest or rental fees.

- Have some or all of your equipment (e.g., computer, fax machine, software) fully or partly subsidised by your employer or claimed back through the tax system.

- Claim tax deductions on household items such as furniture (e.g., desks and chairs) as well as fittings (e.g., curtains/blinds, light fittings and carpets/flooring).

This book will show you what you can legitimately claim back through the taxation system and what is feasible for you to negotiate with your employer for a full or part subsidy.

On the whole, mums who choose to telework stand to gain substantial financial benefits through the reduction of child care, commute and work-related costs. Additionally, there are many potential tax benefits available to eligible teleworkers.

Steps towards teleworking

So how does one go about embarking on a teleworking journey? Teleworking can be achieved by negotiating a suitable working arrangement with a current, prospective or even former employer (if you intend to start working for them again). It can also be achieved if you work for yourself as a business owner, contractor or freelancer.

Successfully securing a telework arrangement with an employer requires a professional, confident and informed approach. After all, this is a business agreement which requires negotiation, acceptance and review. Some primary issues to consider include:

- Are you able to perform your job at home to equal or better standards than you would at your employer's workplace?
- What benefits will your employer receive from your proposed teleworking arrangement?
- What issues or obstacles do you foresee and how do plan to overcome these?
- Are you able to access the equipment, systems, tools and technology that you need to perform your job from home?

Whilst you probably have some idea of the main benefits that teleworking offers you, your proposal should focus on what your employer stands to gain from your planned arrangement. A step-by-step guide to creating a winning telework proposal is provided in Chapter 8.

But, what if your employer says no? Curbing rejection is all about understanding the concerns of business leaders in relation to teleworking. Based on extensive research, I discuss the key concerns afflicting business managers, providing examples of common reasons for objections. I also provide persuasive, informative responses which you can arm yourself with if you are faced with rejection.

Of course, not all employers are open to the idea of teleworking. This book will save you a lot of time and effort by naming the best and worst jobs and industries for telework opportunities. I also provide details of where to find employers who are recognised leaders in the 'family friendly' work space, and showcase some of the programs and incentives they offer.

Life Story: Maria

Teleworking has been a saving grace for me. I experienced difficult pregnancies for both my children. The first time I was stuck in an inflexible job and found myself having to quit. During my second pregnancy I had severe morning sickness for nine months, pelvic problems which rendered me unable to walk, and gall stones. I later developed acute pancreatitis, requiring emergency surgery.

Even so, I was able to work through until five days before I gave birth and resumed my work only six weeks after the birth of my child. Had I been working in a traditional role with a lack of flexibility and inability to telework, I would not have been able to hold down a job at all. For me, this may have resulted in considerable financial strain. Instead, having negotiated a suitable work schedule which involved a full telework option with part-time hours, I was able to work to full capacity. I was also able to resume work quickly and seamlessly after childbirth and also after surgery - without compromising my employer's interests, my health or my family's needs.

www.teleworkingmum.com.au

The power of knowledge

Mothers are a very special breed of people: we are resilient, conscientious, multi-tasking, compassionate, hard-working, unwavering and committed. So why do so many women feel a sense of career inferiority once they become mothers? And why do so many mothers feel as though they can't marry up their family life with a career?

Whilst the culture of the workplace plays a major part in the acceptance and accessibility of flexible work options, your own mindset is the fundamental key to making telework a part of your life. Making the change you desire in your work/life routine is somewhat limited by your own knowledge of what is possible and also by your understanding of how to successfully action your desires.

This book will be an eye opener for many working parents struggling with their traditional nine to five jobs, trapped in uncompromising systems and beliefs. It might just trigger a turning point in your career, opting for a more flexible profession. It may even help you break free from your own chains once you realise freedom lies simply in negotiating a flexible work arrangement with your employer, to the benefit of both parties. Or, it may lead to a complete break from your existing employer in favour of a more family-friendly one who supports true work/life balance. Who knows, you might just find the inspiration you need to go solo by either starting your own business or becoming a freelancer. Running your own show can provide you with the flexibility to make decisions about where, when and how you work.

Flexible workplaces

Many mums often compare their experience of re-entering the workforce as being similar to hitting a brick wall: so many obstacles with no means around them. Some of these obstacles symbolise the inflexibilities that employers present.

Workplaces that foster a vibrant, contemporary place to work, embracing work/life balance, diversity and equal opportunity, thrive as businesses as too do their employees. Workplaces that are stuck in outdated modes of employee engagement struggle with higher staff turnover rates, lower levels of employee satisfaction and generally poorer business performance. Not surprisingly, the morale of employees in these organisations suffers tremendously.

> **Aussie women and parents are among those with the poorest perceived work/life balance.**
>
> *Souce: Pocock et al, AWALI, 2009*

You may be astounded to discover what some employers now offer their employees to attract, engage and retain good talent. In the past, many mums felt a harsh disconnection between their job and their social wellbeing, with no room for family or personal interests. But finally, businesses are slowly, but surely, coming to the fore and obviously listening to what the workforce needs to live and work in harmony. Those businesses that fail to acknowledge these needs and implement strategies to address them will struggle to keep afloat in today's competitive market. Businesses need to redirect their investment towards their greatest asset – their employees.

Teleworking can be introduced by businesses quickly and easily and usually at a low cost and low risk. Many businesses who have implemented teleworking across their workforce show amazing return on investment (ROI) with improvements across multiple major business indicators.

Mums in the workforce

Mums today are doing more paid work than women in the 1960's, yet we are actually spending more time focused on our children now than our foremothers did. This is being achieved through less housework, less sleep, less socialising and more multi-tasking. [2]

Fast Facts - Women in the workforce

- Women comprise about 45% of Australia's workforce
- 45% of women in Australia work part-time
- Labour Force Participation Rates in Australia:
    - All women 58%
    - All men 72%
    - National average 65%
    - Women with children aged 0-4 years 51%

Source: Australian Bureau of Statistics 2009.

---

[2] Ways to Work website (a Victorian government initiative) ways2work.business.vic.gov.au

In Australia about half of women with young children aged 0 to 4 years are engaged in some form of employment, whether this is for an employer or via self-employment. Many mums want or need to re-enter the workforce but are inhibited by lack of flexible workplace models. This lack of suitable work options available to mums re-entering the workforce drives approximately twenty percent[3] to exit to the workforce altogether.

Work provides individuals with an improved state of wellbeing through increased self-esteem, social interaction and financial security. Work also contributes significantly to our sense of personal identity.

Today, women are having babies much later in life and are more educated and more career-oriented than their predecessors. More of us are in managerial and executive roles. Then, as we gear towards the height of our careers – somewhere between the ages of 25 and 35 – we have a baby, or two. We usually leave the workforce temporarily for an average of nine months, most of which is unpaid maternity leave.

Our decision to return to work from maternity leave is largely driven by financial strain. The stresses of today's economic climate make it no longer possible for a family to survive on a single income. For some families, mum's income draws the fine

---

[3] Australian Bureau of Statistics, *Australian Social Trends*, 2007.

line between survival and financial ruin. Some mums are the family breadwinner, whilst some mums are single parents.

An Australian government-sponsored study revealed that higher family income, absence of financial stress and higher parental occupational status were factors contributing to improved wellbeing for children.[4]

Statistics indicate that there are significantly more women than men with a primary care responsibility for children. There is also a much greater proportion of working mothers than fathers adopting flexible work arrangements to meet their caring responsibilities.[5] Recent reports indicate that fathers' employment is largely unchanged by having children.[6]

There is a live source of untapped talent wasting away in our suburbs. Some mothers exit the workforce due to the lack of flexible employment models. Other mums abandon their profession in favour of less skilled jobs as a means of coping with the demands of their caring responsibilities. With the pressing skills shortage our nation is facing, it is time to look at better ways at re-engaging this forgotten treasure and improve our nation's capacity to remain competitive in the global market. Mothers can no longer be ignored as valued members of the

---

[4] AIFS, *Growing Up in Australia Study*, 2008.

[5] ABS 2009. Approximately three quarters of working mothers use flexible work arrangements to care for their children. In comparison, around 40% of male working parents use work arrangements to accommodate their caring responsibilities.

[6] AIFS, *'Parents Who Don't Use Childcare: Who provides the care in working families with infants'*, 2009.

workforce contributing to the strength of our nation's social and economic wellbeing.

Chapter 2

Teleworking Facts

What is teleworking?

Teleworking is not a job; it's a way of working. Teleworking is also known as 'working from home', 'telecommuting', 'cyber working', 'mobile working', and 'e-working'. Teleworking promotes a results-driven work environment where the work you produce is your ultimate measure of assessment.

Teleworking involves two key elements:

1. working away from your employer's workplace, and
2. a technology-enabled work environment (whether you simply use your telephone or go as far as utilising elaborate forms of technology and/or communications).

Teleworking assumes that your commute time is reduced by working away from your traditional workplace. Working remotely can include working from home, at a client's site, at the beach, at an airport, etc. Therefore, if you work from home using your personal computer you are considered to be teleworking, and even if you are lucky enough to be at the beach talking to clients on your mobile phone, you are also considered to be teleworking. For the purposes of this book I will address the home as the main workplace for teleworkers.

'Teleworking' and 'telecommuting' were terms coined by Jack Nilles of JALA International, in the 1970's. He deemed telework as work which is *independent* of location. Therefore, jobs that can be done irrespective of your place of work, e.g., writing, is highly suited to teleworking. However, work that *is* dependent on location, e.g., dentistry, is least suited to telework. Chapter 6 discusses the best and worst teleworking jobs.

There are several categories of teleworkers. This book focuses on the following two:

1. Employee teleworkers who work from home either full-time, part-time or on a casual basis.
2. Self-employed, freelance or contract teleworkers who work from home either full-time, part-time or on a casual basis.

Teleworkers can perform their work mainly from home, or partly from home, i.e., they may attend their traditional workplace for part of the day or week and also undertake some work from home for the remainder of their work routine.

In the early days, teleworking was seen primarily as a solution to greater work/life balance. Today more critical outcomes are being realised through the application of this flexible work-style. Some of these include environmental benefits, the ability to retain and attract valuable talent and considerable financial savings which could potentially improve one's state of economic wellbeing.

What does it involve?

Teleworking involves the use of some form of technology to communicate with your colleagues, customers, suppliers or partners. Teleworkers do not necessarily require a computer or internet access, although many work at home jobs do. This is largely due to the prevalence of technology in modern day society. Technology has become an accepted means of communications across our social and business spheres. The low cost and vast accessibility makes it easier for people from all walks of life to integrate technology into everyday living.

Fast Facts - Teleworking

- In Australia about 2.7 million workers do some of their paid work at home.
- Around one quarter of all employed people undertake some paid work at home.
  - 45% of these are women
  - 41% of these have children under the age of 15
  - Nearly 80% of these are aged 35 years and over
  - 72% of these work 35 hours or less per week
  - 70% of these have an arrangement with their employer to work at home
- Less than 10% of the current workforce work only or mainly from home

Source: ABS, Locations of Work, 2008 and Labour Force, 2009

Who's doing it?

Around 2.7 million Australians are doing some of their paid work from home. The Australian Bureau of Statistics indicates that approximately one quarter (24%) of Australia's workforce telework to some extent.

More than half of teleworkers in Australia are professionals and a good proportion of these are in the higher income brackets. Although almost half of the workforce is made up of women, just over 40% of women undertake some of their work from home.

Why telework?

Teleworking offers many benefits to the home-based worker. For some people this might include more time to spend with family, financial savings, less stress, more flexibility, or more mobility. For mums with young children, however, the benefits of teleworking are compounded, providing multiple positive outcomes.

Mums often experience emotional difficulties leaving their young children in the care of another person in order to work. For me, this was one of the strongest drivers behind my decision to telework. Wanting to experience motherhood to the fullest, and wanting to share my children's early years as much as possible are common sentiments shared by many mothers of young children.

Quite often, mothers of young children find themselves in a better financial position by not participating in the workforce at all. This is usually due to the burdensome costs associated with returning to work such as childcare and commute costs. Teleworking, however, may considerably reduce some of these costs, making it far more viable for parents to return to the workforce.

Teleworking opens up an entirely new dimension to who can participate in the workforce. Without this option employment opportunities would be reduced or non-existent for some families. Thus, teleworking carries strong mobility and flexibility issues as well as immense equal employment opportunity weight.

Benefits of teleworking

The benefits of working from home present attractive incentives for mums, enabling a more seamless integration and better management of work and family responsibilities. However, there are countless other benefits, particularly those associated with considerable time, cost savings, higher levels of productivity, improved efficiencies and better environmental choices.

Teleworking offers mums optimal time with your children to watch them grow and experience every step in their early lives. It also provides the opportunity to contribute to the family's income whilst also maintaining or developing your skills and employability.

Saving money is usually a high priority on mums' agenda, given the added expenses that come with raising a family. Saving money may provide the freedom to work fewer hours each week, resulting in many other ensuing benefits. Teleworking also provides working mums greater flexibility and accessibility.

Whilst there are potentially hundreds of benefits associated with teleworking, below is a list of 20 significant benefits applicable to mums and carers of children:

1. More time
2. More family interaction
3. Better work / life balance
4. Less commute time
5. Reduction or elimination of commute expenses
6. Less stress
7. Ability to return to work sooner after parental or sick leave
8. Making the difference between returning to work and exiting the workforce (employment vs. unemployment)
9. Continuity of skills
10. Maintaining or enhancing employability
11. Reducing your carbon footprint
12. Saving money by reducing work-related expenses such As corporate wardrobe, lunch expenses, social and networking functions, etc.
13. Saving money by claiming household expenses through the tax system: telephone, utilities, rent/mortgage interest fees, furniture, computer, etc.
14. Greater personal mobility (e.g. ability to hold your job whilst traveling or studying)
15. Eliminate or reduce the need for childcare by reducing the hours your child is in child care, or by doing without.

16. Greater flexibility. Opening the gateway for more lifestyle choices. (e.g. rising cost of city living vs. more affordable outer suburbs or regional areas.)
17. Ability to reduce sick leave/absenteeism – more flexibility to look after your children if they are sick; also ability to maintain work throughout your own illness.
18. Higher level of job satisfaction
19. More control over your immediate environment, providing greater levels of personal comfort
20. Increased wellbeing

What benefits hold the greatest value for you? List your top five reasons for wanting to telework:

1. _____

2. _____

3. _____

4. _____

5. _____

Saving time

Time is a critical factor for busy mums. Luckily, it's one of the biggest savers for those who telework. Saving on commute time often amounts to a significant number of hours each week for many working families. For mums, this often results in more time spent with your child, and possibly less time your child is in childcare.

Teleworking can provide the choice to modify the structure of your working day. If you are able to work flexible hours from home you don't need to adhere to the typical business hours of 9 to 5. You can work either very early in the morning or late at night, leaving more time in between to share with your family, undertake study, develop a hobby or do whatever your heart fancies.

The following hypothetical scenario illustrates the significant impact of commute time for an employee traveling to and from a traditional workplace.

Scenario

A typical work day for Lisa consists of the following commute times:

- Dropping kids off to childcare (15 minutes)
- Driving to work (1 hour)
- Driving back to childcare (1 hour)
- Collecting kids and returning home (15 minutes)

www.teleworkingmum.com.au

- If Lisa works full-time, she spends 12.5 hours per week commuting, equal to 27 full days per year.

- If Lisa works three days a week, she spends 7.5 hours per week commuting, equal to 16 full days per year.

- If Lisa teleworks, she spends zero hours commuting. Therefore Lisa potentially saves between 360 and 600 hours per year by teleworking. (That amounts to between 16 and 27 full days of the year!)

How much time do you spend commuting to your job each day? Try this quick quiz.

Time to get to work: _____

Time to get back home: _____

Total pick up and drop off time for childcare: _____

Now add all three figures together to get the total number of hours you commute each day.

To work out how many hours you commute each week, multiply this total by the number of days you work per week.

To work out your annual time savings multiply the total number of weekly hours saved by 48 (assuming you take 4 weeks annual leave).

Business benefits

There are many benefits for employers who offer telework. From a businesses perspective, teleworking can be a significant driver of growth, productivity and business efficiency.

The enormous cost of corporate overheads, particularly real-estate expenses, creates an attractive incentive for many businesses to implement telework programs for suitable employees. There are also other spin-off benefits which are derived from creating happier employees who have greater work choices, an improved work/life balance, less stress and an increase in job satisfaction. These can range from increased productivity, greater employee loyalty, lower staff attrition rates, higher staff retention rates and higher job satisfaction levels.

Many studies have confirmed that teleworking increases productivity levels for businesses. The main underlying factors for this include: reduced absenteeism and improved levels of job satisfaction.

Life Story

A small Melbourne based internet marketing firm expanded its business by choosing to re-invest most of their profits in their workforce. They did this by opting to bypass real estate and infrastructure costs. The company closed their city based headquarters and employed quality staff on a permanent telework basis, enabling them to increase their manpower from two to fourteen home-based contractors. The contractors were required to provide basic business tools including a computer, internet connection and an email system. This saved the company thousands of dollars each month.

www.teleworkingmum.com.au

In an economic downturn the benefits derived by cutting significant costs through telework arrangements makes a positive impact on the overall economy. It means fewer jobs get cut, recruiting new employees is more viable, and businesses are able to stay afloat by making huge cost savings on major overheads such as real estate leases, utility costs and other major infrastructure expenditure.

In the case of natural or man-made disasters (for example the September 11 terrorist attacks), teleworking can provide an effective means of business continuity, establishing a defence for disaster recovery. Similarly, in cases of a pandemic outbreak, implementing telework in businesses would allow for a seamless transition in work location, ensuring continued and uninterrupted business.

Nortel Australia implemented a telework program within their business over ten years ago. As a result they are experiencing savings of approximately $40 million per annum on real estate / facility costs and telephony expenses.

Key business benefits

- Increased business efficiencies and cost savings
- Reduced absenteeism / sick leave
- Higher rates of employee satisfaction
- Higher levels of productivity
- More opportunities for regional businesses
- Business continuity in cases of pandemic, natural or man-made disasters
- Greater support for disaster recovery

www.teleworkingmum.com.au

- Shorter parental leave time
- Ability to retain knowledge base
- Increased opportunity to retain skills base
- Significantly lower overheads
- Lower attrition rates
- Reduced expenses on staff hire rates
- Be recognised as employer of choice
- Ability to attract the best talent
- Ability to hire staff across a greater geographical spread
- Be seen as an innovative business
- Offer improved Equal Employment Opportunities

The following table lists some key business improvements achieved by organisations who have implemented teleworking. The statistics indicate the percentage improvement experienced, on average, across multiple businesses.

Improvements	Statistics
Improved productivity	By up to 40%
Increased employee effectiveness	Around 12%
Reduced absenteeism	By up to 80%
Reduced sick leave	By at least 2 days per annum per employee. A Morgan and Banks study found that sick leave was costing Australian businesses $2.56 billion per year.
Reduced attrition rates. The cost savings include re-hire, advertising and re-training costs associated with staff turnover.	Reduce avoidable staff turnover by around 20%. It costs around .75 and 1.5 times an employee's salary in replacement costs. The higher skill level, the higher the cost. Senior managers and executives can cost up to 2.5 times their annual salary in replacement costs. It also takes up to eighteen months to retrain new recruits to the same level of knowledge as the employees who they replaced.

Community benefits

> **Teleworking can save Australia 3.1 million tonnes of carbon emission savings per year**
> (via reduced traffic congestion alone).
> *Source:* www.climaterisk.com.au

There are significant community benefits that can be gained from teleworking. Teleworking provides long term sustainability for the country's economic and environmental wellbeing. For example, some areas which can benefit from adopting long-term teleworking practices in Australia include:

- Reduced pollution and carbon emissions (from reduced traffic congestion and inner city utilities overload)
- Less demand for national roads/infrastructure expenditure
- Sustainable national employment levels
- Improved business continuity in times of natural (or man-made) disaster
- Prevention or reduction of a proportion of road traffic accidents and fatalities
- Improved road traffic for non-teleworkers, emergency response units and the general community
- Increased access to more work opportunities for rural and remote communities
- An overall improvement in community social, economic and environmental welfare.
- Improved equal employment opportunities.

Obstacles to teleworking

Whilst there are endless benefits that teleworking offers, it's not all a bed of roses. There are some points to consider carefully when deciding on whether or not teleworking is right for you and / or your employer. Like the benefits, the obstacles to teleworking may not be applicable to everyone who teleworks, but they are certainly worth bearing in mind. It's also important to understand that some teleworking issues or obstacles can be overcome by careful planning and preparation. The following discusses some of the main concerns affecting some teleworking parents or employers and offers suggestions to overcoming these.

For teleworkers

Time management is a critical factor for teleworking parents that can either make or break your journey. Trying to coordinate a work schedule whilst also having the responsibility of supervising your children can be challenging. There are, however, some simple key ingredients to finding a solution to overcoming this obstacle.

Having a good routine that is well prepared, realistic and achievable is one of the key points to overcoming barriers to a mum's time-deprived schedule. Careful consideration of the needs of your employer and your family must also be factored into your planned routine.

For most working mums this usually entails either enlisting in some form of child care help (formal or informal), and/or taking on a smaller, flexible work load. I managed ten hours' work a week from home quite comfortably with minimal child care help. When children enter toddlerhood they become more active which means that they usually require less daytime sleep and they also become more accident prone, requiring constant supervision. At this point in my teleworking journey I relied on occasional child care assistance to manage my paid work during business hours. This provided up to three hours of care which fitted in well with my two hours per day work requirements. On the days my children did not attend occasional care I sometimes split my work into two one hour sessions (morning and evening) – particularly for specific tasks which involved heavy concentration.

Tips for optimising time management:

- Plan ahead. Map out your work routine to ensure you are ready to jump straight in, ensuring you have all the necessary tools, information, etc., you need.

- Ease into teleworking slowly. Take on a small number of hours per week as a trial to see how this pans out. One to two hours of work per day can be weaved into your routine with greater ease, and possibly with less reliance on child care, if that is what you prefer. Greater work hours will almost certainly mean you will need to enlist in some form of child care help – be it formal or informal. Teleworking is not an automatic substitute for childcare.

- Power work during opportune times. For example, if your child has a midday nap, or if someone is available to relieve you of your caring duties, use that time wisely to maximise productivity, without unnecessary interruptions.

Isolation can sometimes present as a significant obstacle to teleworking. Not being in face-to-face contact with your colleagues or clients makes it difficult for some people to cope. If you're a highly social person who thrives on people interaction, then teleworking may not be the right choice for you. There are, however, certain steps you can take to circumvent the feeling of isolation during your teleworking journey.

Attending meetings at your workplace on a regular basis can often provide a good source of face-to-face interaction with your colleagues or clients. However, many individuals who thrive in teleworking arrangements don't feel isolated at all and actually prefer to attend meetings via teleconference, instead of commuting to the office to attend in person.

Another alternative is to attend your work's premises for part of the week then telework the rest of the week. Remember, you don't necessarily need to give up your 'at work' component in full, if you don't want to. Allowing provision in your telework agreement for a review may provide you the opportunity to either reduce or increase the proportion of 'at work' hours versus the hours you work 'at home' if and when you need to.

For Employers

Trust

There is often a perceived difficulty amongst managers in monitoring and supervising employees who telework[7]. This

---

[7] Toshiba, *Mobility and Mistrust*.

issue can be effectively addressed by developing organisational measures based on performance rather than attendance. For some roles it may require an analysis of which job components can be teleworked and which ones are unsuitable. Developing a set of goals or deliverables that can be documented and measured can provide an effective solution to overcoming issues of mistrust.

Security

Security is the second main obstacle encumbering telework adoption in business. Security issues include:

- Secure systems for sensitive documents/materials
- Removal of sensitive documents, e.g., personnel records
- Privacy compliance
- Adherence to company security processes

Most of these issues can be prevented or managed with effective processes and security based technology, which most businesses generally deploy for organisational protection (regardless of whether or not their employees telework). Most security breaches are due to human error (e.g., leaving your USB stick in a public place), rather than acts of malicious intent.

Process

There is a need for workplace policies on teleworking. Policies provide a set, clear outline of how, when and who can telework in your place of work. Once established, the process can be followed without the need to re-invent the wheel every time someone embarks on a teleworking journey. Policies also help set expectations on who can telework as well as outline the exact procedure required to submit a telework proposal and initiate a telework plan.

Useful References

- Telework Australia – www.teleworkaustralia.com.au

Chapter 3

Financial Benefits

Saving money

For many mums, the financial benefits derived from telework have a significant impact on their decision to return to work. By reducing many of the costs associated with returning to the traditional workplace – particularly for families of young children - teleworking can positively impact your life and your family's wellbeing.

So, how much money would you save if you teleworked? Reducing commute and child care costs alone can make an enormous difference to most families' budgets. Other immediate savings for teleworkers can include expenses for petrol, parking, toll fees, lunches, tea breaks, social club, wardrobe, grooming, gifts, donations, wear and tear of car, and many more.

The table below illustrates some of the main financial savings that a teleworking mum could potentially make. It also shows that for mums with a primary care responsibility of pre-school aged children, there is a large difference in the cost of returning to a traditional workplace, as opposed to teleworking.

Scenario: Jane is returning to work as a Project Administrator, for fifteen hours a week, spread across three days. She is concerned that the high cost of childcare and commuting may override any gains she is hoping to make from working. She is now considering approaching her employer about teleworking to cut back on these costs. Here is a summary of Jane's expenses based on the two scenarios:

(a) working at her employer's workplace, and

(b) working from home:

(a) Work at employer's workplace weekly expenses:		(b) Work at home weekly expenses:	
Petrol	$ 22	Petrol	$ 0
Parking	$ 34	Parking	$ 0
Childcare fees	$ 224	Childcare fees	$ 0
Lunch	$ 15	Lunch	$ 5
Wardrobe	$ 30	Wardrobe	$ 0
Other - wear & tear of car, social club, gifts, grooming.	$ 30	Other - internet subscription, phone line & other incidentals	$35
TOTAL	**$355**	**TOTAL**	**$40**

Jane earns around $543 per week (net), based on working part-time (3 days per week).

Scenario (a) – If Jane attends her employer's workplace she stands to lose around $355 of her income to childcare fees and

www.teleworkingmum.com.au

work-related expenses. She is eligible for the government's rebate for childcare, so she will be reimbursed 50% of these costs. This changes her weekly expenses to a total of $243. Jane will therefore be pocketing around $300 per week by returning to work three days per week at her employer's premises.

Scenario (b) – If Jane teleworks, the majority of her weekly expenses will be eliminated. If Jane is able to spread her work hours across her week to enable a more flexible routine she will be able to work around her family whilst also canceling out the need for formal childcare.

Commute and parking costs will also vanish, leaving Jane with only a small weekly cost of internet subscription and telephone costs. These costs can be claimed legitimately via the taxation system as work-related tax deductions. Therefore Jane's weekly expenses for working at home are almost negligible. Jane will pocket at least $503 per week, saving a minimum of $203 per week, by teleworking. That's a saving of over $10,000 per year!

What does your job cost you?

Take the following short quiz to work out:

(a) **What it would cost you to return to work at your employer's premises, and**

(b) **What expenses would be reduced or eliminated if you teleworked.**

(a) If I work at my employer's workplace these are my weekly expenses:		(b) If I work at home these are my weekly expenses:	
Petrol	$	Petrol	$
Parking	$	Parking	$
Transport fees	$	Transport fees	$
Childcare fees	$	Childcare fees	$
Lunch	$	Lunch	$
Wardrobe	$	Wardrobe	$
Other	$	Other	$
	$		$
	$		$
TOTAL	$	TOTAL	$

Saving tax

Teleworking blends the boundaries of your home and work spaces. In effect, this can potentially create greater scope for savings via the tax system. As a teleworker, you can make legitimate tax claims for many home expenses if you can validate these as a means to support your home based work. This can make quite a difference to the dollars that could end up in your pocket at the end of the financial year!

Planning is key to maximising the tax benefits that teleworking offers. To some degree, you have the power to influence the extent of your savings by establishing the best possible framework for your home based work. The way in which you set up your home working area, to the proportion of time you work from home, as well as your employment status (i.e., whether you are an employee or business owner) all play important roles in affecting your tax savings.

Whilst in some ways your home expenses might increase because you work from home, e.g., power and telephone usage costs, some expenses are often fixed costs and don't increase simply because you work from home, e.g., property rental expenses, telephone line rental, light fittings, floor coverings, etc. By working from home, many of these items may be claimable as tax deductions or depreciation items. If you don't work from home these costs would be additional costs to the household budget.

Now, just because you work from home does not automatically qualify you for claiming relevant household expenses as tax deductions. The delimitations prescribed by the taxation system provide different types of tax deductions for the various levels of work from home situations.

The following is a basic guide to what you can legitimately claim through the taxation system when you telework. Please consult with your taxation advisor/accountant or the tax office for more details, as each individual taxpayer's or business owner's circumstances may vary.

What you can claim

When working from home as an individual taxpayer or as a business owner, you are entitled to claim on two main groups of expenses:

1. **Home office running expenses** - this includes utilities such as gas, electricity, telephone.

2. **Home office equipment and furniture** – this includes the cost of purchasing and maintaining office furniture such as desks, chairs, etc., as well as equipment such computers, faxes, printers, etc. If you don't claim on the cost of purchasing these items, you might be able to claim on the depreciation – i.e., the decline in value, for the life of the item. You might also be able to claim on items such as flooring (e.g., carpet, rugs), window furnishings (e.g., blinds, curtains) and light fittings for costs, repairs or depreciation.

Following is a description of each of the main expenses that are considered either running expenses or relating to home office equipment/furniture.

Utilities. These expenses are the main group of costs relating to the running of your home based work space. These include gas and electricity costs. You can only claim on a portion of your expenses, representing the fraction of floor space used for work /business, in proportion to the rest of your home. To work out what your gas/electricity usage is for your work area calculate the size of the floor space for the room(s) you utilise for work and use that fraction to apportion your full utility bill.

You can calculate your exact portion of your utilities bills and depreciation costs or you can opt to use a set rate provided by the tax office for the financial year that you incurred these expenses (e.g., 26 cents per hour). This will cover depreciation costs, gas and electricity costs. For example, if you elect to claim using the set rate of 26c per hour, by working 20 hours per week you can claim $5.20 per week as 'running costs'. This saves you the hassle of having to calculate each individual item, although, for some teleworkers, this might be less than the actual expense incurred.

Telephone expenses. Teleworkers can claim on work/business telephone usage and line rental but not installation costs. If you use one telephone line for work/business and personal calls you will need to keep a record of your business calls and work out the proportion of the bill that you can claim. The tax department uses the following formula to decide on what proportion of calls can be claimed via the tax system:

Work or business calls (incoming and outgoing) / Total calls (incoming and outgoing)

Depreciation costs of office plant and equipment (e.g., desk, chairs, computer, printer, etc.). It is important to note that if your equipment (e.g., computer) is used for personal use as well as for work purposes you will need to apportion the expenses accordingly. You can also claim depreciation costs for room fittings such as carpet, curtains and light fittings if you have a dedicated work room or area that is utilised exclusively or mainly for work purposes.

Cleaning costs of your home office. This includes any professional cleaning services you might enlist, cleaning equipment hire (e.g., carpet steam cleaning machine hire), detergents, cleaning tools, etc.

Repairs / maintenance costs of your office furniture or equipment. This includes repair or maintenance of any of your office equipment and furniture, so long as it's used for income generating purposes. For example, computer servicing, re-upholstery of damaged office chairs, replacement of equipment parts, etc.

Occupancy expenses

A third category of household expenses, called 'occupancy expenses', allows provision for some teleworkers to claim on some major household expenses (such as mortgage interest/rental fees, home insurance premiums, etc). The costs associated with owning or renting your property may be claimed as legitimate tax deductions by eligible teleworkers if your home is considered within the tax guidelines as your main place of work/business. Occupancy expenses include:

- Rent or mortgage interest fees
- Home insurance premiums
- Council rates
- Water rates
- Repairs & maintenance (relating to entire house, not just parts of the house, e.g, painting and repairs to gutters)

Claiming on occupancy expenses, however, can be a little complicated. Traditionally, occupancy expenses applied mainly to business owners and it was only on rare occasions that employees would satisfy all the requirements in order to legitimately claim these expenses.

With the surge in telework, however, some employees now find themselves with no other option but to work from home. For example, some employers stipulate that it is a requirement of the job to work from home. Some employers operate virtual workforces with no dedicated headquarters, whilst some employers are based interstate. Therefore, for these employees, the home is the main place of work out of necessity, not just by choice. In these situations occupancy expenses might be claimable, depending also on your home work space setup. The tax department will not allow occupancy expenses to be claimed by employees who work from home simply out of convenience.

If you are able to claim on 'occupancy expenses' you will need to claim on the fraction of floor space used for your work/business in proportion to the rest of your home. Therefore, if you use a workshop plus a room for office space you will need to add the floor space of these areas and claim on that portion of your expenses. Usually, this should not exceed 30% of your total home area. So if your total work area amounts to one fifth of your home, then you can generally claim on one fifth of your relevant household expenses.

When claiming home occupancy expense deductions, or using your home as a place of business, you may be liable for capital gains tax when (or if) you sell your home. This would apply for the portion of your home declared as a place of work/business and would apply for the period you operated for. Consult with your tax advisor or the tax office for more details.

Another important point is that if you fall within the tax department's 'Personal Services Income' (PSI) category, you might not be able to claim on occupancy expenses.

Personal Services Income (PSI). Many freelancers, contractors and consultants operate their business either as a sole trader, company, trust or partnership. It is important to understand whether or not your income is classified as 'Personal Services Income' (PSI), as categorised by the tax department.

In general terms, Personal Services Income is income derived from your 'labour' (including skills, knowledge and expertise), as opposed to income for 'materials' (including products, tools or equipment) used. If 50% or more of your income is derived from your labour efforts, then your income is most likely to be classified as PSI.

If the PSI rule applies to you then this may limit the tax deductions which you can claim. For more information please refer to the *'Personal Services Income'* section on the Australian Tax Office's website: http://ww.ato.gov.au.

The Australian Taxation Office has an online calculator for working out how much you can claim on household bills when you work from home whether you are an employee or self employed. Visit http://www.ato.gov.au (see 'home office expense calculator').

➢ Keeping a diary to support your tax claims

When claiming home office expenses (especially as an individual tax payer) you will be required to keep a diary for at least four weeks to support your tax claims. This will show the proportion of time your office space and / or equipment has been utilised for work (income generating) purposes as opposed to personal usage. As a minimum, the details recorded in your diary should outline the dates and times of day that you utilise your home office or work area for work related activities. For example:

> **Date: 14 May 2010   Start: 9:00am   Finish: 3:00pm**

You can apply the total hours you calculate from your sample four weeks to the remainder of the year, allowing for periods where your home office is not utilised for work (i.e., when you are on leave, sick or not working).

➢ Where is your main place of work or business?

The tax system provides more extensive tax benefits for those whose home is classified as their main place of work/business, as distinct from those who use their home only occasionally to undertake work/business activities. There are also more tax benefits on offer when you have a dedicated work room or work area in your home. This means that this space is utilised either exclusively or primarily for income generating purposes, and is therefore used sparingly for personal use.

The following tables outline the expenses you may claim as tax deductions:

Summary - expenses you can claim via the taxation system when your home *is* your main place of work.

Expenses Claimable	*If you have dedicated work room or area*	*If you do not have a dedicated work room or area*	*If you run your business from home*	*Notes*
Telephone costs	✓	✓	✓	You can claim on line rental and call costs but not on installation costs.
Utilities: gas, electricity, etc.	✓	✓	✓	
Depreciation costs of furniture & equipment	✓	✓	✓	
Depreciation costs of office area fittings	✓		✓	
Repairs & maintenance to your office furniture / equipment	✓	✓	✓	

www.teleworkingmum.com.au

Continued....

Summary - expenses you can claim via the taxation system when your home *is* your main place of work.

Expenses Claimable	If you have dedicated work room or area	If you do not have a dedicated work room or area	If you run your business from home	Notes
'Occupancy Expenses,' i.e., the cost of owning or renting your property. E.g., rent, mortgage interest fees, home insurance, council & water rates.			✓	These expenses can be claimed when your home is your main place of work or business. However, if you are an employee, consult with your tax advisor to see if you qualify to claim on these tax deductions. If your income is classified as PSI you cannot make these tax claims.*
Repairs & maintenance to home			✓	Generally if you can claim on occupancy expenses you can also claim on these expenses.

* Check with your tax advisor or the Tax Department.

Summary - expenses you can claim via the taxation system when your home is _not_ your main place of work/business but you do some work from home (e.g., after hours or on occasion).

Expenses claimable	You have dedicated work room/ area	You do not have a dedicated work room/ area
Telephone costs	✓	✓
Utilities: gas, electricity	✓	✓
Depreciation costs for furniture and equipment	✓	✓
Depreciation costs for work area fittings (curtains, carpets & light fittings, etc)	✓	

You cannot claim for occupancy expenses (e.g., rental costs, mortgage interest fees, insurance, rates etc.,) as your home is not considered your main place of work or business.

Scenario

Jenny works from home as a Marketing Assistant. She works as an employee for 20 hours per week. Her home is her main place of work and she has a dedicated room which she uses solely as her home office. The room size represents approximately 15% of the entire floor space of her home.

Jenny's employer covers the cost of her telephone calls by providing her with a mobile phone which is fully subsidised. Jenny has also been supplied with a laptop and all the software she requires to do her work. Here is an example of what Jenny may be able to claim as home office tax deductions for the current financial year:

Expenses	Details of Possible Expense Claims
Internet subscription	Jenny uses approximately 20% of her internet subscription for personal use and the remainder for work purposes. Therefore Jenny can claim up to 80% of her total bill as a legitimate tax deduction.
Utilities: gas, electricity, etc.	Up to 15% of all utilities bills.
Depreciation costs of furniture & equipment	Depreciation costs of office furniture, including office desk, chairs, bookcases, filing cabinets, etc. Depreciation costs for any equipment used for work that is owned by Jenny, such as printer, fax, etc.
Depreciation costs of office area fittings	Depreciation costs of fittings in dedicated work room, including: carpets, rugs, window furnishings, etc.
Occupancy expenses	Jenny is not able to claim on these as tax deductions as she is an employee who chooses to work from home for her own convenience.
Repairs & maintenance to home	These expenses are generally tied in with 'occupancy expenses' and are mainly claimable by eligible self employed people or employees who qualify.
Repairs & maintenance to office furniture / equipment	Jenny can claim on most costs relating to repairs or maintenance to the office furniture and equipment that she owns and uses for work. This includes servicing costs, repairs or replacement of parts.

This chapter outlined the types of expenses that you might be able to reduce or eliminate by teleworking, as opposed to working in a traditional workplace. It also discussed the household items and expenses that can be claimed via legitimate means through the tax system. The extent to which your home can benefit in this manner will depend largely on:

(a) your work area
(b) your employment status (i.e., employee or self employed)
(c) the degree to which you telework

As a word of caution, you should use the information provided in this chapter as a basic guide to the tax and financial savings that you might be eligible for. The taxation system is complex and has many variations to each rule, depending on each taxpayer's circumstances. Therefore, you should consult with your accountant or tax advisor to ascertain the exact deductions that apply to you.

Useful references

The Australian Taxation Office - www.ato.gov.au
See the following topics:

- Home Office Expense Calculator
- Personal Services Income
- Small Business - Home Based Work Essentials

Chapter 4

Returning to Work

> **Fast Facts – Returning to work**
> - About 5% of women return to work within days or weeks after giving birth (AIFS, 2008)
> - 10% of women return to work within 3 months after giving birth and over 50% return when their child is 1. (ABS, 2008)
> - 25% of women take no maternity leave (some of whom quit their jobs when their baby is born).
> - 14% of women plan to leave the workforce to have children (EOWA, 2008)
> - Almost half of mothers with children aged 0-5 are engaged in the workforce (ABS, 2009)

Returning to work after having a baby is a huge decision families often need to face. It's a complicated issue, loaded with immense emotional weight, vital financial implications and stressful logistical hurdles. Consequently, returning to work often raises a stream of questions and concerns for parents: Will I return? When will I return? A new job or an old job? Full-time or part-time? How do I negotiate flexibility? Should I start my own business? What are my childcare options? Can I afford childcare? How will we cope with separation anxiety? Is it worth returning (especially considering my income after childcare expenses)?

Like most things associated with parenthood, there is no right or wrong answer. Your own circumstantial needs, your preferences and available options will all influence your decision to re-enter the workforce. Some mums are forced back into the workforce due to financial strain, whilst others make the choice to do so – whether it's to maintain employability and skills, to make a contribution to the family's income, or for other personal reasons. Research has proven that a fulfilling job can instill a positive self identity, confidence and an increased sense of self esteem.

This chapter provides a simple breakdown of the many pieces that make up the return to work puzzle. By untangling the key issues that often afflict parents, it aims to help you form a clearer perspective on your objectives of returning to work, providing a solid framework for developing your return to work plan.

Drivers and benefits

If your head feels clouded with a myriad of thoughts and concerns about returning to work, it might help you to know that you're not alone. Most families go through the agonizing process of deciding when, how and where mum will return to work.

Sorting through your thoughts, emotions and the practicalities on this issue might take some time. However, to help you along your way, this chapter provides a practical approach to help you develop some sense of clarity and purpose. Defining your needs and desires is the first step towards achieving your goal.

Fleshing out your thoughts on paper often helps you achieve a sense of direction. It also provides a good reference point to return to and revise when and if you need to. Following is a set of questions which is best used as a workbook. Write down your responses to the questions and feel free to return to your responses at any time and revise them if you need to.

1. Understand your reasons for returning to work.

Financial gain remains a high motivational factor for many mums returning to the workforce. However, many women simply seek the fulfillment that a career or job can bring.

Write down the five main reasons why you want or need to return to work:

1. _____

2. _____

3. _____

4. _____

5. _____

2. Pinpoint the benefits of returning to work.

Would you work if there was nothing to gain from doing so? Probably not! For many mums this question imposes a blatant reality check. Documenting what your perceived or expected benefits are from returning to work can serve as a checkpoint when you re-engaged in the workforce, to see if it all pans out as expected.

What do you expect to gain from returning to work?

1. _____

2. _____

3. _____

4. _____

5. _____

3. Establish a timeframe to return to work.

Whilst it's not always possible to return to work when you ideally want to, it's important to establish a point in time that is at least workable within your own agenda. Most mums approach this timeframe issue from the perspective of their child's age group.

I would like to return to work (tick one):

☐ When my child is 0 – 3 months

☐ When my child is 3 – 6 months

☐ When my child is 6 months – 12 months

☐ When my child is 12 months – 18 months

☐ When my child is 18 months – 2 years

☐ When my child is 2 years – 3 years

☐ When my child is 3 years – 5 years

☐ When my child is in school

☐ Not sure

4. Identify your preferred job avenue.

Re-entering the workforce after either having a baby or being out of the workforce for some time can create different needs, limitations and desires. What was once an ideal job may now fail to hold the same benefits or appeal as it once did. Now is a good time to evaluate what you want to do with your career and decide whether you want to continue in the same line of work, change employers or start your own business.

I would you like to return to work (tick one):

☐ To my existing job

☐ To a new job with my current employer

☐ To a new job with a new employer

☐ As a self-employed business owner/freelancer/contractor

www.teleworkingmum.com.au

5. Confirm your availability and preferred work style.

The next sets of questions helps you work out how you would prefer to work, to what extent and what your availability is.

1. **I would like to return to work (tick one):**

   ☐ On a full-time basis

   ☐ On a part-time basis

   ☐ On a casual/temporary basis

   ☐ On a contract basis

2. **I would like to incorporate the following flexible work arrangements in my role** (tick as many options as you like):

   ☐ Telework (work from home)

   ☐ Part-time or casual

   ☐ Compressed hours (working longer hours to reduce number of days)

   ☐ Flextime (flexible start & finish times)

   ☐ Job Share (when two part-time staff share a full-time role)

   ☐ Flexible leave options

   ☐ Other

3. **I am available or willing to work the following days/hours per week:**

   _____

   _____

www.teleworkingmum.com.au

4. I would like to telework (work from home) during these days/hours per week:

_____

_____

5. I would need to attend my employer's workplace during these days/hours per week:

_____

_____

The aim of this exercise was to help you understanding the why, when, where and how of returning to work. These basic, yet essential, details help you set the foundations for a positive return to work journey. You can re-visit your answers at any time and make changes as you need to. Knowing what's right for you is what will make your transition back to work an easier and more pleasant experience.

The cost of returning to work

The costs associated with returning to work often create significant barriers to re-entering the workforce for parents of young children. This can be a major inhibitor of workforce participation for those with a primary care responsibility for children.

Therefore, knowing what these costs are is crucial in the process of deciding whether or not to return to work. Also deciding on how many hours and what form of flexibility to propose to your employer may also be swayed by what it will cost you to return to work.

The following set of questions can be answered twice:

(1) Assume you return to your existing job, or a traditional job.

(2) The second time assume you incorporate some degree of telework into your work schedule. Then, compare the two.

1. **What childcare arrangements would you require or choose?**

   ☐ Informal – family or friends

   ☐ Long day care

   ☐ Occasional care

   ☐ Family day care

   ☐ Nanny / babysitter

   ☐ Pre-school / kindergarten / school

   ☐ None

   ☐ Other _____

2. **What will childcare cost you each week?**

   _____

3. **Are you eligible for a government or employer sponsored child care rebate/subsidy?**

   ☐ Yes

   ☐ No

4. If yes, deduct this rebate from your child care costs and write the revised cost amount here (per week):

5. Considering any changes to your return to work conditions (e.g., change in hours, change in role, etc.,) what will your net income be (i.e., after tax) each week?

6. What work related costs will you need to pay for?

Item	*Weekly $ Cost*
Public transport fees...	
Petrol fees..	
Parking fees...	
Wardrobe costs..	
Grooming costs (hairdressing, etc)......................	
Lunch / amenities costs.......................................	
Car repairs & maintenance costs.........................	
Subscriptions or licenses.....................................	
Technology costs: - internet................................	
- telephone..	
- other	
Stationery costs...	
Insurance costs..	
Other costs..	
....	
....	
TOTAL...	

7. What will it cost you to return to work? Add the totals of your child care costs (item 4) with the total of all other work related costs (item 6).

8. To work out what your income is after all your work related expenses, including childcare fees, take your weekly net income amount (item 5) and deduct the total of your return to work costs tallied in point (7). What amount are you left with, if any?

This exercise helps you work out the financial aspects of returning to work. For some parents, the costs associated with returning to work defeat any financial gains you expect to make. Ensure you do your sums to work out if returning to work is feasible for you.

Childcare

One of the main reasons mums find teleworking so appealing is because it alleviates some of the pressures of finding, securing and paying for suitable childcare. Whilst working from home might not completely eliminate the need for childcare, it could possible reduce your reliance on it, or allow you to optimally manage your work/life schedule for better facilitation of your childcare arrangements.

Childcare can be quite a stressful issue for parents of young children. The cost is high, securing your preferred type and location of service is not always possible and separation anxiety (for both child and parents) can be tough.

Some mums I have spoken to have indicated that, based on their income levels, the high cost of childcare (especially long day care) makes re-entering the workforce inaccessible to them. Even with the government childcare rebate, costs are relatively high. This is particularly the case for families with more than one pre-school aged child and/or lower income earners.

Teleworking does not automatically cancel your need for childcare. Yes, it can provide you with a great deal of flexibility and freedom to work around the needs of your family. However, depending on a number of factors surrounding your work requirements, you may still require some form of childcare help – be it formal (e.g., long day care) or informal (e.g., other family members).

Even after having secured suitable childcare arrangements, there needs to be a reasonable degree of flexibility built into your work routine to manage times when children get sick or need to stay home. If telework was woven into your usual work routine you would be able to seamlessly manage your work at home at times of need.

It is important to understand what childcare options are available to you. The Australian government maintains a website providing a central point of information for all your childcare issues (including other useful information on raising children in Australia). Visit **www.mychild.gov.au** or refer to your local council for a list of all childcare services in your area.

Life Story - Carla

Last year I investigated the possibility of placing my toddler in long day care for one day a week. I was working from home on a part-time basis but had recently increased my hours to fifteen hours per week.

As it turned out all the local childcare centres were booked to full capacity - all but one, so I made an appointment to see the centre and meet the staff.

This particular centre had been in the media about their financial troubles and it had clearly affected their reputation in the market. When I attended the centre for an inspection I found that what were normally two separate rooms was now one room consisting of 3 year olds, 4 year olds and 5 year olds, plus their numbers were that low they still had vacancies.

As much as I had faith in the centre and trusted that they would care for my child to their best ability I was not comfortable placing my child in an environment steeped in stress. The staff were under a lot of pressure and feeling insecure about the future of their jobs and their workplace, which no doubt would be sensed by the children in their care. I couldn't place my child in such an environment. I did not apply for a place at this centre but put my name on the waitlist for three others.

Eighteen months later, Carla was still waiting for an available place for her child. The childcare centre with vacancies went into receivership and subsequently went out of business.

www.teleworkingmum.com.au

Fast Facts - Childcare

➤ In Australia about 711,000 children use formal childcare. About 45% of these attend long day care. A further 1.1 million children use informal child care such as relatives and other people. (ABS, 2008)

➤ About 65% of families using formal child care do so for work-related reasons. (ABS, 2008)

➤ There has been a 35% increase the in the number of children attending childcare in Australia over the past ten years.

➤ A federal government census report in 2008 revealed that over 10,000 children in Australia were in day care for 50 hours or more per week.

A research study of 100 Australian children in day care revealed that the stress hormone cortisol was found in higher levels for those children attending centres with lower standards and also increased throughout the day.

Do I need childcare?

As a teleworking mum, whether or not you will require childcare assistance will depend largely on the following factors:

The type of work you do. Some jobs can be undertaken with minimal social interaction. These types of jobs can often involve a high degree of computer work and may also incorporate other facets of technology such as internet, databases, specialised software, etc. These jobs are well suited to telework and also offer greater flexibility for when and where you can undertake your work. Therefore, integrating your work schedule around your family's routine is somewhat easier. On the other hand, a job with a high level of social interaction – whether it is by phone or face-to-face – is more restricting. Work times are usually less flexible as you usually need to make yourself available during set hours, and this largely depends on business hours or customers' preferences. Therefore, flexibility is limited. This translates to a greater probability of requiring child care assistance to perform your job satisfactorily. The same applies to jobs that demand a high degree of focus and undivided concentration.

The number of hours you work – generally, the fewer hours you work, the less reliance you will have on childcare. This is because fewer hours can be integrated into your family's routine more easily. As a mother of two pre-school aged children, I find working ten hours per week manageable. I work two hours per day across five days per week. I don't take on any additional work unless I have the flexibility to do it during my 'free' time, i.e., late in the evenings, during my children's afternoon nap time, or on weekends when other family members can supervise my children. It wouldn't be viable to work full-time hours and look after a child/children concurrently, without some form of childcare help.

The degree of job flexibility – it is important to negotiate expected work times and routines with your employer. If you are able to work flexibly around your family's routine then this allows you more freedom to choose times that suit you. If, however, you are required to work set hours during the day then the reliance on childcare services increases considerably.

The ratio of time you telework – as opposed to the percentage of time you need to attend your workplace. Usually, if you attend your employer's workplace, provision for childcare assistance is essential for preschool children. For the ratio of work that you undertake from home, a combination of the issues discussed above will come into play.

The availability of an adult to supervise your child while you work – Many mums opt to work flexibly around their partner's work routine and have them mind the children when they return home from work or during their rostered days off. Researchers have dubbed this practice 'shift-parenting', where parents take turns in caring for their children in shift-like routines in order to accommodate their job requirements as well.

If childcare is not an option for you, a smaller, manageable number of work hours per week will allow you more flexibility to supervise your kids sensibly and responsibly.

Scenario

Emily has a one year old daughter and has two part-time jobs which she undertakes mainly from home. Both jobs require Emily to work 10 hours per week, totaling 20 hours per week. This is how she manages her schedule:

Job 1: 9-11:00am (2hrs) x 5 days per week = 10 hours

Job 2: 8:30-10:30pm (2hrs) x 5 days per week = 10 hours

TOTAL = 20 hours per week

Job 1 requires Emily to work during standard business hours. Emily elected the 9-11am time-slot as this is the time her baby usually has her morning nap. Job 2 can be undertaken at any time and therefore Emily allocates two hours every evening once her baby goes down for her evening sleep, or her partner is available to take over the child caring responsibilities. Therefore, even though Job 1 needs to be done during set hours, the small number of hours Emily has committed to means that it is more achievable within her family's routine.

Emotional hurdles

> **About one in ten working women feel guilty about having their child in child care.**
> *Source*: Raising Children Network. http://raisingchildren.net.au

Many working mothers experience a strong sense of guilt or sadness upon returning to the workforce. Quite often this is compounded by separation anxiety which their children experience but which they may also experience themselves.

Emotions associated with guilt tend to escalate initially when you first make the transition back into the workforce. For many mums these feelings ease off as you and your child become accustomed to your new work/life routine. Children develop better coping mechanisms as they get older, so they are less likely to experience separation anxiety, say at the age of four or older. This also depends on previous exposure to using childcare services.

If you find that your guilt or sadness does not ease over time, it might be worthwhile reviewing your working arrangements. Perhaps you could work more hours from home or perhaps work fewer hours altogether. It might take a few trial variations until you finally get it right. Furthermore, from an emotional wellbeing perspective, it may be worthwhile speaking with a counselor, maternal health nurse or your family doctor.

Separation anxiety can be quite overwhelming for both child and parents. It is quite a natural reaction to leaving your child in care, or even school. Experts say it commonly occurs in children from six months to two and half years, although it can extend until a child is four years of age.

There are several things you can do to cope with separation anxiety and improve the process of leaving your child in care:

1. **Explore** your child care options and choose one that suits you. Visit the centre with your child several times to see if you both feel comfortable with the setting, the staff and the quality of service.

2. **Inform** the caregiver with information about your child's routine, likes/dislikes and fears so that they are able to maintain a consistent pattern to accommodate your child's needs.

3. **Trial.** Keep your child in care for a shorter period during the first few days to ease into his new routine.

4. **Plan** the night before so that you can start your day in a relaxed and positive manner. Being rushed and disorganised can often spark feelings of anxiety or anger.

5. **Say goodbye.** Always say goodbye to your child and reassure them that you will be back at the end of the day. Say it only once and then make your exit. Leaving without saying goodbye to your child destroys trust.

6. **Reassurance.** It doesn't hurt to give the centre a call during the day to check in on your child. It's not, however, a good idea to turn up to the centre at any time between drop-off and pick up times unless your child will not see you. If your child sees you and you don't intend to take your child with you, it is likely to disrupt the day and cause your child unnecessary distress.

Building your confidence

I think most mums would agree that being away from the workforce for an extended period – whether it's ten months or ten years - makes you feel a bit jittery about returning. Lack of confidence for mums re-entering the workforce might be attributed to some or all of the following issues:

1. Personal changes, including: physical, emotional, familial and motivational.
2. Change in your responsibilities at home and possibly at work.
3. Change in the way you are perceived by peers/managers (actual or assumed).
4. The gap in your resume. How do I explain my time out of work attending to parental duties?
5. Dealing with changes since last being employed, e.g., technology, processes, personnel, skills and knowledge.

Returning to an existing job or employer

Returning to the same employer can be just as daunting as re-entering the workforce via a new job or employer. So much can happen in a short span of time: changes in staff, policies, practices, technology and so on.

Being out of touch with these changes can make you feel disadvantaged to some degree. If you are on maternity leave it would help considerably to keep in touch with your colleagues, team or managers to overcome this issue and avoid feeling overwhelmed upon your return. There are many ways you could achieve this:

- **attend team meetings**
- **receive email updates**
- **catch up with colleagues for informal catch-up sessions over lunch or coffee**

Returning to a new job or employer

For some mums, the experience of workforce re-entry via a new job can often be a refreshing option, allowing greater scope to carve out your role in a way that's more congruent with the changes in your life.

Life Story - Bianca

Becoming a mother can empower women in so many ways. For me, it gave me the courage to stand up and reclaim my worth as a woman. After several failed attempts at re-entering the workforce as a first-time mum my confidence level was at an all-time low. But then, as I began to question my worth, it suddenly struck me: hey, I have a tertiary qualification plus over a decade of industry experience under my belt, with a host of glowing references. I've worked hard to achieve this and no-one can take that from me, nor can they down-play my achievements simply because I now have a child. If anything, becoming a mother is a step up in my line of achievements, certainly not a step down.

It's important for mums to take a step back and reclaim their worth, rather than wither away or allow their confidence to diminish them.

www.teleworkingmum.com.au

Positive steps towards workforce re-entry

1. Polish up your resume
One of the most common concerns for mums re-entering the workforce via seeking a new job is the question: "How do I explain the gap in my resume?" The answer is to translate what you have been doing into business savvy terms. 'Highly organised', 'multi-tasking', 'marketing skills', etc. Have you helped your partner with their work or business? Have you done any voluntary work? But don't just state what your skills are, provide examples of how you have developed these skills, or used them to benefit an employer, customer or organisation.

2. Practice business talk and prepare for interviews
It's amazing how quickly you can lose touch with work by being away for any length of time - particularly when most of your conversations have been with a baby! Polish up on your business talk and practice before attending interviews.

3. Dust off your work wear or invest in new ones
Looking the part is feeling the part. Sort through your wardrobe for a decent outfit then have it dry cleaned and ready for your interview. Even better, if your budget allows, invest in a smart new outfit to help boost your confidence. Some women experience a change in their bodies after giving birth so it's worth the investment for an improved level of confidence and self esteem.

4. Research your market
Know what kinds of jobs are out there and develop your own 'wish list'. Draw up a list of types of roles you would like to do

and then matrix them back to the skills and experience you possess.

5. Interview tips

Don't ramble about your children or family. Focus on selling yourself by matching your experience, skills and knowledge to the position. If you have been out of the workforce for a while, use some savvy business talk to tell your interviewer(s) about some recent experience or skills that you have acquired. For example, if you have done some volunteer work for your local charity functions tell them you have been involved in promotion, marketing and event management roles.

6. Resume tips

Omit personal details on your resume. Again, as per the previous point, focus on your skills and experience and don't include personal details such as date of birth or marital status – they are simply irrelevant.

7. Discussing flexibility

Discussing flexibility with an existing employer is usually a bit easier and less daunting than with a new or prospective one. However, if you are applying for a new job and prefer to work part-time hours or would like to incorporate a telework component, make sure you clearly communicate this as early as possible.

If you are entering the market via a recruitment agency, specify your needs, limitations and desires about the job you are seeking. It doesn't hurt to enquire about full-time jobs when your skills and experience are a good fit, yet you are only available part-time hours. State this at the outset and see whether the recruiter can persuade the employer to consider you. However, make it clear that you don't want to waste your time or theirs if they are not willing to take you on with a reduced work schedule.

Whilst it might not lead to any immediate results, it's worth asking about flexibility in the interview. This will help you gauge whether the employer offers flexibility to its existing workforce, or whether they are open to this in the future. If they have a flexible working policy in place, then this is a good indicator of their attitude towards these practices.

In some instances, negotiating flexible work styles such as telework might need to be delayed until your new employer gets a chance to know you. As a guideline, consider the provisions offered by the new Fair Work Act. This suggests that flexibility becomes open to negotiation for eligible parents/carers who have had a minimum of twelve months' continuous service with the same employer. This serves as a good guide for when it might be appropriate to start negotiating with your employer.

However, if telework is a necessity for you, search for jobs that indicate that there is scope to perform your job from home.

Life Story - Linda

It was only 6 months after the birth of my first baby when I started to look for work again. Emotionally I wasn't ready; I wanted to be at home with my baby, yet due to financial strain I was forced to find a job.

The job ad was for an Administrator for a Management Consulting firm in the city. I was very excited and called the employment agency. I was invited for an initial interview after which the consultant highly recommended me to the employer. The same day I got a call back. Success! The interview was tomorrow at 9am. I called mum and arranged for her to come and baby sit.

It had been well over a year since I last had a corporate job, so I wasn't sure what to wear. As I searched my wardrobe I knew I was in trouble. I had only just stopped breastfeeding so my breasts were a lot bigger than they used to be and my belly and hips were very bloated. I ended up with an uncoordinated outfit - a mix match of anything 'corporate-style' that actually fit.

Cont...

... cont

Albeit, the interview seemed to go really well. The three interviewers appeared impressed by my skills and experience, but everything started to crumble as we moved on to a sensitive topic. They asked me how I felt about returning to full-time work after having a baby.

"Ideally I would like to work three or four days initially and then extend this to full-time at a later stage," I said. The interviewers threw darting glimpses at each other and one of them shifted her stance to a crossed-arm position. I sank in my chair. "I made this clear to the employment agency that I would prefer to work part-time for the next few months...they said you would consider it." They looked at each in confusion again and said that the role was full-time and that was their preference.

My heart sank. I sat there emotionally deflated, the tears swelled in the back of my eyes. What a waste of a lot of effort and precious time.

The lessons learned through Linda's experience is that she may not have made it clear enough to the employment agency who communicated with the prospective employer that she was temporarily limited to working part-time hours. If you are set on certain needs – such as availability - then this should be relayed

www.teleworkingmum.com.au

to the people with whom you discuss future employment opportunities. Don't be afraid to re-affirm your requirements if you feel any aspect of this has been ignored or misunderstood.

8. Networking tips

Get the word out and let everyone know that you are seeking employment. Online job boards, family, friends, neighbours – expand your opportunities through traditional and non-traditional networking channels.

9. Study

Many mums take the opportunity to study whilst on maternity leave, or away from the workforce. Whether you are re-skilling, or upskilling, take advantage of the many training courses now available via flexible and / or distance learning methods. It's a great way to stay in tune, improve your skills or learn new ones.

10. Government grants

Research the internet to find out if your state government provides any return to work or study grants for parents. Check out the following:

VIC - Victoriaworks – financial assistance up to $1000 for parents returning to work after two years of caring for your children. Grant can be used for study, books, childcare fees, transport, etc. Visit:

www.parentsreturningtowork.com.au

ACT – ACT Return to Work Grants are open to women returning to the workforce after twelve months of caring for their child. Financial assistance of up to $1000 is available.

The program is funded through the ACT Office for Women, ACT Department of Disability, Housing and Community Services and is administered by the Women's Information and Referral Centre (WIRC). Visit:

www.dhcs.act.gov.au

Useful References

➢ www.earlychildhoodaustralia.org.au

➢ www.mychild.gov.au

➢ www.parentsreturningtowork.com.au

➢ www.dhcs.act.gov.au

Chapter 5

The 'F' Word (Flexibility)

'Flexibility' is no longer a dirty word. The Australian Government has recently put its official stamp of approval on flexibility for parents in the workforce, with the introduction of the landmark Fair Work Act.

Eligible working parents now have the right to request a change in their working arrangements to allow greater flexibility to balance work with their caring responsibilities. In a nutshell, as a parent of young children you now have the right to request flexibility from your employer and your employer has a duty to respond to your request.

> **In the UK around 50% of employers offer teleworking and around 89% offer part-time work.**
>
> This is largely due to UK legislation which entitles parents of young children the right to request flexible working arrangements from their employer. Since the introduction of the 'right to request' legislation in 2003, it is reported that the majority of requests for flexibility have either been fully or partially accepted (at least 90%). Only a small number of claims reached the industrial relations tribunal.

Your right to flexibility – new laws explained

From the 1st January, 2010, Australia introduced workplace legislation under the Fair Work Act as administered through the National Employment Standards (NES). The NES provide ten enforceable minimum employment standards, or entitlements, that are applicable to employees within the national workplace relations system. (To find out if you are covered by the national workplace relations system visit **www.fairwork.gov.au**.)

There are two specific entitlements within this new scheme which are directly applicable to working parents:

a) Parents who have at least one child under school age, or a disabled child under the age of 18, now have the right to request flexible working arrangements from their employer.

b) The second entitlement provides the right for a minimum of 12 months' unpaid parental leave, with the right to request an additional 12 months of unpaid leave.

Eligibility

Working parents or carers of children who are under school age have the right to request a change in their employment conditions to incorporate some level of flexibility to enable them to care for their children. Parents or carers of disabled children under the age of 18 may also be eligible. The other criteria you must also meet to make you eligible for this new work entitlement is that you must have had more than twelve months of continuous service with your employer and this must be immediately before making your request. This legislation covers full-time, part-time and casual employees.

What kinds of flexible work arrangements can I propose?

There are no set guidelines or limitations to what 'flexible' work arrangements you can propose. When considering your flexible work arrangements you should be mindful of what would be reasonable and viable from your employer's standpoint.

What is considered a 'reasonable' flexible working proposal?

There are no guidelines provided by the government because every employer, every role and situation can vary extensively. You need to apply logic when considering your flexible work request and perhaps offer your employer an explanation of how your proposed working conditions will suit them and also provide details of how you will implement this.

An example of a proposed flexible working arrangement may include one or a combination of the following:

- a change in the hours of work (either working less hours, or a change in start or finish times, compressed hours, etc.)
- a change in the location of work (e.g., working from home)
- a change in the way in which you work (for example, job share).

An outline of some prominent flexible work options are provided in the next section of this chapter.

How do I request a flexible working arrangement?

There are two requirements for employees who wish to submit a request for flexibility to their employer:

1. Your request must be made in writing.
2. Your written request must include details of why you seek flexibility.

Consider providing a response to the following two questions:

(a) What change to your current working conditions are you requesting?

(b) Why are you requesting this change?

NOTE: *Chapter 8 provides details on how to prepare your proposal.*

What obligations does my employer have?

Employers are obligated to respond to your request for flexibility in writing within 21 days of receiving this. They are, however, not legally obligated to accept your proposal and can refuse this on reasonable business grounds. If your employer refuses your proposal they must provide reasons for this in their written response.

What are reasonable grounds for refusal?

Whilst there are no set criteria for 'reasonable grounds of refusal' some of these might include:

- The nature of your role and its suitability to telework or other flexible work styles
- The likely impact your request will have on the business
- The likely impact your request will have on your team
- Inability to provide resources/skills/staff to service your request
- The cost to the business

Therefore, if you feel you have a good case for incorporating flexibility into your role, it would be a good idea to address the above issues in you proposal – or any other issues you feel might be raised by your employer.

What if there is a dispute?

Whilst there are no current avenues for arbitration, the government has established these new workplace standards based on international practices which provide evidence that by simply inviting these conversations between employees and employers, we improve our channels of communication. This invariably leads to improved working conditions down the line.

Fair Work Australia - the national workplace relations tribunal - is empowered by the Fair Work Act 2009 to hear workplace disputes where there is a formal agreement or contract in place. Therefore, unless your flexible working arrangements are formalised under a contractual agreement, this new legislation acts simply as a promoter of workplace discussion and negotiation, but does not offer a means of arbitration.

Bear in mind that it is unlawful to discriminate in the workforce against individuals with caring responsibilities and there are both state and commonwealth laws to protect individuals against this. In Australia, a number of cases have been heard by courts or tribunals on these issues, some of which include parents returning to work after parental leave who have been refused flexibility by their employer. In certain cases the tribunal ruled in favour of the employee, because it was ruled that the employer did not exhaust all avenues to find alternative arrangements in order to provide the employee with their preferred flexible work request.

Discrimination laws protect individuals who are being treated unfairly. Within the workplace, discrimination laws cover you when you are applying for work or in the way you are treated at work. For parents or carers, there are specific types of discrimination laws which can protect you:

- Pregnancy discrimination – being treated unfairly because you are pregnant.

- Breastfeeding discrimination - being treated unfairly because you are either breastfeeding or expressing milk.

- Carer's discrimination – being treated unfairly because you have caring responsibilities (either for children, an ill, disabled or elderly family member).

Where to get help:

If you feel you are being discriminated against in your workplace, speak to your Equal Employment Opportunity representative or contact the Fair Work Ombudsman or visit their website for further information:

www.fairwork.gov.au

Your guide to flexible work options

A flexible working arrangement is one where you and your employer jointly negotiate a suitable work-style plan to suit your needs as a working parent whilst also meeting your employer's business needs. This may involve a change in location, work hours, or the way in which your work is carried out.

Telework is one form of various flexible work syles. There are many other flexible work options which can also be incorporated into your work routine, in combination with telework or on their own.

Following is a list of various flexible work options that have been adopted by many Australian workplaces. The great thing about flexibility is that it can be woven into your work routine when you need it most but can later be modified or ceased if your needs or your employer's needs change.

> **Telework**

Working from home or away from your employer's workplace is called teleworking. You can choose to telework for your entire work schedule, or part of it. Therefore you can negotiate full work at home arrangements with your employer or a combination of home-based and work-based hours, depending on what's feasible for you and your employer. You can telework permanently, casually, or on a contract basis.

> **Part-time**

Working part-time is generally working less than the full-time work hours[8]. Part-time workers are permanent employees with reasonably predictable work hours. Entitlements such as annual leave, sick leave, etc., are provided on a pro-rata basis.

> **Job Share**

Job share means two or more part-time employees share one full-time job. Job sharing arrangements can be made where there is a need for full-time hours to complete your job successfully, yet you are only available to work part-time hours.

> **Flexible working hours**

This is also known as 'Flex-time' or 'Flexi-time' by some workplaces. This involves flexible start and/or finish times e.g., leaving work early and logging on at home in the evening, or another example might include working late one day and leaving work early another day.

Some employers set the number of hours to be worked per week or per month and allow the flexibility for staff to work these hours when it suits them. Some employers offer their employees core work hours that must be worked within a specified part of the day or week, and then allow staff to undertake the remainder of their work hours flexibly.

---

[8] Generally, 38-40 hours per week is considered full-time employment, although some work places consider 35 hours a full-time week.

> **Flexible roster or shift work**

This involves developing a change in your roster or shift work to allow adequate flexibility to accommodate your parental caring responsibilities. For example, you might want to work extra hours in the month leading up to school holidays then roster on for less hours during the school holiday period.

> **'Hours bank' or 'make up time'**

An 'hours bank' is where any additional hours you work are 'banked' for you to use flexibly at a later date when needed. Some workplaces allow employees to use these hours to leave early, start late, or as annual leave time. 'Make up time' works similarly, where leaving early or starting late can be logged on a register whereby you can opt to 'make up' these hours at a later time.

> **Compressed working week**

A compressed working week is working your required work hours throughout a compressed period within the week. For example, a work schedule of 28 hours per week could be worked over three days, instead of three and a half days.

Working compressed hours makes a lot of sense for many parents who rely on formal child care services (especially long day care centres where fees are charged per day – regardless of how many hours your child is in care for.) Using this flexible work mode could reduce the days your child is in care, thus reduce your fees and commute hours as well.

www.teleworkingmum.com.au

➤ Flexible leave options

There are various flexible leave options that can be implemented to allow workers more time to achieve work/life balance. One common practice amongst workplaces today is to allow staff to 'purchase' leave.

Permanent employees are entitled to annual leave benefits. The minimum entitlement is four weeks' annual leave for full-time employees (or five weeks for some shift workers). Part-timers receive a pro-rata entitlement. Some workplaces offering 'purchased' annual leave will allow up to a further four weeks' annual leave which then requires a readjustment of wages to reduce the overall salary by the equivalent of four weeks' pay. This is sometimes referred to as working 48/52, where the salary received is 48 weeks out of the 52 weeks of the year.

➤ Annualised working hours

This working arrangement is usually based on the seasonal or fluctuating demands of the business. Staff are generally paid their regular wages throughout the year, although they may be able to work fewer hours or days during 'quieter' periods to compensate for an influx of work which may require additional hours or days during the 'busy' seasons.

➤ Contracting

Contracting can offer a great deal of flexibility for workers and employers. Contractors can generally choose where and when they work, allowing them considerably more flexibility than employees. However, contractors are not employees; they are self-employed individuals who have different legal and financial reporting (taxation) obligations. Some workplaces expect contractors to supply their own tools and equipment. On the flipside, some workplaces allow provisions for certain tools or equipment for contractors in their hourly rate, thus providing a higher rate of pay.

The Australian Taxation Office website provides more details on how to distinguish between an employee and contractor, and also provides details on what obligations a contractor has. It also outlines the various deductions you can claim when working as a contractor. Visit:

www.ato.gov.au

When choosing a suitable work style, consider several flexible working arrangements simultaneously. For example, telework, part-time and job share are three flexible working arrangements that can easily be integrated into your routine, at the same time. Any new working arrangement should remain flexible enough to factor in future changes to your needs or your employer's needs. Chapter 8 discusses how to document your plan and approach your employer with a winning telework proposal. However, before you start working on this, the next chapter helps you assess whether or not teleworking is the right choice for you.

Useful References

➢ Your right to flexibility: www.fairwork.gov.au

➢ Your guide to flexibility: DEEWR - The Department of Education, Employment and Workplace Relations (the lead government agency providing national leadership in education and workplace training, transition to work and conditions and values in the workplace). Visit: www.deewr.gov.au

➢ Your guide to obligations and entitlements as a contractor: www.ato.gov.au

Chapter 6

Is it Right for You?

Whether you work for an employer or run your own business, most teleworkers usually thrive in their home-based working environment. Reports have shown that teleworkers are more productive than their 'at work' colleagues. They usually experience a higher degree of job satisfaction and therefore an increased sense of dedication to their work. The autonomy aspect is also a highly desirable element for many teleworkers.

However, teleworking is not for everyone. Quite often the work is done in isolation with limited or no social interaction with the outside world. The hours are odd, usually late at night or early in the morning while the family is sleeping, unless you enlist some form of child care help. Working from home also requires loads of dedication and self discipline.

Following are some typical traits that are common amongst successful teleworkers:

1. **Enjoy autonomy** – If you prefer to be micromanaged, working from home is not for you. You must enjoy taking ownership of the job to get the work done efficiently and to your best ability with little or no supervision.

2. **Self disciplined** – Whilst working flexibly means you can make adjustments to your schedule to fit in other responsibilities or interests, you need to demonstrate a strong sense of self discipline to avoid unnecessary distractions and to commit to your schedule and promised work deliverables.

3. **Motivation** – You need loads of it!

4. **Dedication** – to getting the job done professionally. Teleworkers are typically assessed by the results they produce, not by the hours they attend their workplace.

5. **Organisation** – This is a critical telework ritual. From keeping your work area organised to keeping a diary, planning ahead and scheduling sensible and achievable work goals is crucial to a successful telework journey.

6. **Dependability** – Your employer and/or customers need to feel confident that they can depend on you to get the job done – regardless of where you work.

7. **Tech savvy** – Working from home often entails using some form of technology. Whilst this might be as simple as email or the internet, feeling comfortable with technology and having knowledge of basic troubleshooting tips will enhance your teleworking experience and curb unnecessary time wasting.

8. **Satisfaction** – If your heart's not in it you will struggle. After having a baby many mothers find a renewed outlook on life partly due to their change in priorities, but also because of the break away from their workplace. Mums often find themselves re-evaluating their job or career during this phase of their lives. Decide what you really want to do. Maybe it's time to start your own business, do something more creative, or

perhaps you'd like to study or start on a new career path. Whatever it is your heart desires, go for it!

Best & worst Industries for teleworkers

It is difficult to place clear boundaries around each industry with regards to their suitability for teleworking. Each industry has its own share of job functions that are both very well suited to teleworking and those that are poorly suited to teleworking. However, certain industries maintain a greater proportion of telework opportunities, whilst others have a greater tendency to maintain more job roles that are unsuitable for teleworking arrangements. This is primarily due to the concentration of job types that make up each industry.

Keeping in mind that there are exceptions in every industry, the table below is a general guide to the best and worst industries for finding telework opportunities.

Best Industries for Teleworking Opportunities			
Information Communications & Technology	Government	Professional and Business Services	Health Services

The Information Communications and Technology (ICT) industry is one of the leading industries adopting teleworking practices. This is mostly due to the ubiquitous (meaning widely available) nature of technology that exist for mobile workers within this industry.

Government organisations are leading implementers of technology in Australia. This, coupled with the Government's acknowledgement and support of flexible workplace practices, make this industry one of the teleworking leaders.

The Australian Bureau of Statistics reports that a significant proportion of teleworkers are from a Professional Services background. These are usually the kinds of jobs that can be done with minimal supervision, and can be done almost anywhere, irrespective of location.

The Health Services industry is an interesting one in that a great deal of jobs in this industry are people-facing, for example health professionals such as General Practitioners, dentists and other health providers. This makes it highly unsuitable to telework. However, there has been a considerable shift in recent years in the service delivery models for this industry. Many health and allied services are now delivered remotely such as via the telephone or the internet. This is particularly the case in many remote areas where patients are not able to physically attend a clinic due to health or distance reasons. The same trend is also taking effect in the Mental Health arena whereby counseling sessions are delivered via telephone, video or web conferencing.

The other aspect of the Health Services industry which lends itself to being well-positioned for telework is its large component of support roles that are highly suited to flexibility and working from home. These include administration, research, analysis, planning, strategy, transcription services, etc. This industry has a great proportion of these types of roles.

Worst Industries for Teleworking Opportunities		
Hospitality Retail	Manufacturing	Construction

The industries least suited to telework are generally very location-dependent, with a high degree of customer-facing requirements, or rely on heavy/industrial machinery or equipment. Workers in these industries generally need to be physically present at a dedicated work location to service customers, e.g., hospitality and retail, or to use the tools/equipment to get their job done, e.g., construction and manufacturing.

Due to the nature of the construction and manufacturing industries, i.e., large machinery, noise, pollution, etc., this kind of work is usually restricted to industrial-zoned areas. There are strict by-laws which prohibit most manufacturing businesses from operating in residential areas, and therefore homes. However, some small-scale manufacturing might be suitable to be undertaken from home, for example, clothing. Check your local council regulations regarding any form of manufacturing you plan to undertake in your home.

Best & worst jobs for teleworkers

There are many different kinds of jobs that you can do from home. Generally speaking, work that can be done or delivered using technology such as the internet or computer software is very suitable for a home working environment. Work that has an extensive customer-facing aspect (eg retail sales) or reliance on plant /machinery (eg manufacturing) is least suitable for the home worker.

With today's advances in technology many jobs that were once confined to offices can now be delivered as effectively – if not better – from home. Voice over IP (VOIP) technology, delivering telephony via the internet allows for call centre type work to be easily undertaken from home, or other remote work places. For example, Help Desk roles are suitable to be undertaken from home as each task is logged onto the HelpDesk system, allowing for easy tracking and service level measurement. Similar too are receptionist and other telephony related roles.

The following job functions are considered ideal for teleworking:

Administration	Editing
Analysis	Evaluation work
Architectural/drafting	Marketing
Calculating	Reading / proofreading
Communications	Research
Computer programming	Record keeping / filing
Data Entry	Technology design and support tasks
Database Management	Transcribing
Designing / graphics / artwork	Word processing
Dictating	Writing

The table below illustrates major job clusters that are ideal for telework. Some jobs may require a combination of telework with attendance at an employer's or client's work site, for full optimisation.

www.teleworkingmum.com.au

Jobs suited to telework

Office Support Roles

Administrator	Clerical Worker	Secretary	Data Entry
Bookkeeper	Accounts Clerk/Manager	Personal Assistant	Executive Assistant
Sales Support			Receptionist

Professional Services Roles

Accountant	Business Analyst	Researcher	Strategic Planner
Architect	Draftsperson	Policy Analyst/Planner	Market Researcher
Advertising	Interior Designer		Social Researcher
Project Manager	Risk Manager	Knowledge Manager	Academic
Commercial Analyst	Interpreter/Translator	Statistician	Human Resources Consultant
Engineer			

Creative Services Roles

Artist	Graphic Designer	Fashion Designer	Desktop Publisher
Designer	Illustrator	Pattern Maker	Writer
Art Director	Photographer	Editor	Journalist
Web Designer			

Community Services Roles

Case Manager	Volunteer	Social Policy Analyst	Community Relations Manager
Project Assistant/Manager	Roster Administrator		

Sales and Marketing Roles

Advertising Manager	Marketing Coordinator	Brand Manager	Telemarketer
Public Relations	Events Planner	Promotions	Communications Manager/Assistant
Marketing Executive	Market Research	Sales Consultant	Media Buyer
Lead Generation		Business Developer	

www.teleworkingmum.com.au

	Financial Services Roles		
Financial Planner Stockbroker	Insurance Consultant/Broker	Risk Manager Superannuation Consultant	Mortgage Broker Underwriter
	Building Industry Roles		
Architect Town Planner Draftsperson	Landscape Designer Home Decorator	Feng Shui Consultant Estimator	Contracts Administrator Property Manager
	Legal Services Roles		
Legal Secretary Legal Advisor	Patent Attorney Law Clerk Private Investigator	Legal Transcriptionist Lawyer, Solicitor	Legal Writer Legal Researcher
	Home Services		
Ironing Services	Laundry Services	Caterer	Events Planner
	Cottage Industry Services		
Sewing Candle Making	Aromatherapy Gift Cards	Giftware Jewellery making	Crafts Knitting

A good way to determine whether or not your job is suited to telework is to dissect it into its respective job functions. This will allow you to pinpoint any problems which may hinder its suitability to telework.

For example, an **Office Administrator** might have the following job functions:
- Word processing
- Diary management
- Accounts payable / receiveable
- Time sheet administration

- Email communications
- Data entry
- Dictating

All these job functions are ideal for teleworking, based on the recommendations outlined in the previous tables.

Self assessment survey: is teleworking for you?

Take this short survey to determine if teleworking is suitable for you. The survey considers some key aspects of your job, your personality, your home workspace and your support network.

➢ **My Job**

1. My primary job function involves (tick one)
   - ☐ planning, research, writing, analysis, reviewing, reporting
   - ☐ client or staff interaction, training or face to face services
   - ☐ access to heavy machinery or plant equipment

2. My secondary job function involves (tick one)
   - ☐ planning, research, writing, analysis, reviewing, reporting
   - ☐ client or staff interaction, training or face to face services
   - ☐ access to heavy machinery or plant equipment

3. My job can be done:
   - ☐ At any time of day or night
   - ☐ Within business hours only
   - ☐ At very limited times only

➢ **My Personality**

4. I need social interaction at work
   - ☐ Hardly at all
   - ☐ Sometimes
   - ☐ All the time

5. I prefer to be micromanaged
- ☐ Hardly at all
- ☐ Sometimes
- ☐ All the time

6. I am self motivated
- ☐ Most of the time
- ☐ Sometimes
- ☐ Hardly at all

7. I am easily distracted
- ☐ Hardly at all
- ☐ Sometimes
- ☐ All the time

➢ My Workspace

8. My workspace at home is:
- ☐ A dedicated workspace in a separate room, e.g., I have my own home office.
- ☐ A dedicated workspace in a shared room, e.g., my workspace is permanently situated in the living room/ kitchen/ dining room.
- ☐ A temporary workspace in a shared room, e.g., kitchen

➢ My Support Network

9. I have help caring for my child/children
- ☐ Via formal support (childcare/kinder/school)
- ☐ Via informal support (family/friends/relatives)
- ☐ I don't have any help

10. My family and friends are supportive of my work from home arrangements
- ☐ To a great extent
- ☐ To some extent
- ☐ Not at all

www.teleworkingmum.com.au

How to work out your score

There are ten questions/statements in the survey. Each question has a choice of three responses. The first response option appearing at the top for each question is worth 3 points. The second response option is worth 2 points and the last response option, at the bottom of each set of responses, is worth 1 point. Add up all your points to determine your total score.

Example:

1. My primary job function involves (tick one)

   - 3 ☐ planning, research, writing, analysis, reviewing, reporting
   - 2 ☑ client or staff interaction, training or face to face services
   - 1 ☐ access to heavy machinery or plant equipment

   Your score for this question would be 2

Interpretation of scores

If your score is between 25 and 30:

It appears that you have most of the necessary ingredients to make teleworking a success. It is likely that you can telework successfully for most or all of your job.

If your score is between 18 and 24:

Teleworking may be possible for you, although you may need to make some adjustments to improve your likelihood of success. Pinpoint any areas of weakness and see how you can improve on these. Explore different ways of teleworking, for example, you might telework for part of your work requirements and then attend your employer's workplace to complete tasks that might involve direct people interaction/access to machinery or equipment, etc.

If your score is between 10 and 17:

Teleworking will be a challenge for you to achieve successfully. Identify the areas that are hindering you and see if these can be modified in some way to enable a better chance of success in your teleworking quest. Dissect your role, identifying aspects that can be done from home whilst performing the remainder at your employer's workplace. If your job is significantly inflexible, would you consider changing your job or employer?

If your personality is the major inhibitor then consider the aspects that are creating the barriers. For example, if you enjoy social interaction, would a work-around solution such as scheduled weekly meetings create a sufficient fix?

Possessing a genuine desire to work from home is an essential trait for successful teleworkers. If you are longing to return to the workforce mainly for the face to face social interaction, then teleworking is not for you.

Chapter 7

Telework Opportunities

Nowadays there are more and more genuine home based work opportunities with great flexibility advertised online and in newspapers daily. There are also many hidden opportunities waiting to be discovered. The trick is knowing what to look for and where to find it!

Employers are now realising the benefits of keeping their employees happy and are offering telework and other flexible work options as part of their rewards mix. Aside from retaining valuable personnel within their organisation, these incentives are giving employers a distinct competitive advantage, helping them attract the best new talent.

If you're on the market for flexible work it's important to understand the various avenues available to you. It's not always the obvious or usual channels that hold the best opportunities. Whether you're currently employed and looking for a change in career path or employer, or you've been out of the workforce for an extended period of time, this chapter discusses some of the many job search paths worth pursuing.

1. Approach your current employer

If you are currently employed or on maternity leave, it's generally easier to approach your existing employer, as opposed to convincing a new employer to work from home. One of the biggest issues most employers find challenging is the issue of trust. However, once you've proven yourself in a role it is easier to modify that role by undertaking some or all of it from home.

If you are happy with your current employer approach them about the possibility of teleworking. If your current job is not completely suitable, think about specific parts of this that could be undertaken from home. Alternatively, if your current job is entirely unsuitable for telework, consider discussing a new job with your existing employer – one that is more amenable to telework. Chapter 8 discusses how to prepare a telework proposal, and how to best handle the initial approach and negotiation stages.

2. Approach a past employer

Past employers are great contacts for new work opportunities as you have already proven yourself with them and they are familiar with your work style, skills and knowledge. Having moved on from there you no doubt have additional experience and perhaps new skills to now offer.

Sieve through your past contacts and identify those worth pursuing. Arrange a catch up meeting and let them know where you are at and what you would like to do. If they are open to the idea, prepare a formal proposal and arrange a suitable time to discuss this with them in more detail.

3. Find a new job

For various reasons, you may find yourself looking for a new job. You might be opting for a career change or you might have been out of the workforce for some time. Whatever the case is, when seeking a new job with an element of flexibility, it's important to understand where the streams of opportunities lie and how to best approach them.

    a. **Online job portals.** These days fewer jobs are being advertised in print media, such as newspapers, as the cost and accessibility of online portals provide greater reach and lower costs for advertisers. It also provides a real-time connection with job seekers.

    There are a handful of dominant job search sites in Australia, including the following:

- www.seek.com.au
- www.mycareer.com.au
- www.careerone.com.au

    There are also many niche online jobs boards which specialise in helping mums return to work or finding flexible jobs. Some of these include:

- www.lifestylecareers.com.au
- www.careermums.com.au
- www.mumsatwork.com.au
- www.hiremymum.com.au

There are also many other online jobs boards which provide either broad or specialised employment services.

The Australian Government has created an official online job website to incorporate the many legitimate and valuable sites available for job seekers. This initiative is called JobSearch and is Australia's largest free online jobs website. It contains links to many independent job search websites with information about the kinds of jobs each site specialises in. Check it out:

http://jobsearch.gov.au

b. **Print media.** This includes newspapers, bulletins, newsletters and magazines. Whist the numbers of job ads in this medium are waning, it's still worth your while to take a look if you're serious about finding work. Local and regional newspapers can provide good prospects for job seekers in addition to the mainstream ones.

c. **Internet.** Research the internet and shortlist employers you would like to work for. Sometimes jobs boards are a great eye opener for the kinds of organisations that are employing, and can also provide insight into the kinds of flexible work options offered by individual employers. You might not find the job you are after, but might stumble across an organisation that interests you. Employers who are genuinely 'flexible' or 'family-friendly' openly advertise this aspect in order to entice new employees to their organisation. If your interest is particularly keen, make contact with them and ask to send them your resume for consideration of any future jobs that might come about.

Various government websites provide details about specific employers who are recognised as 'family friendly'. There are also various awards for employers who are leading the way in implementing family friendly programs within their business or organisation. These are particularly helpful as they provide details of case studies, outlining the nature and extent of their flexible work practices. More information on this is provided in Chapter 9, Family Friendly Workplaces.

> **CAUTION! Your online reputation is as important as your offline one.**
> Employers and recruiters are now using the internet and social media sites to research and scrutinise job candidates. So be mindful of this when posting comments, photos/videos online.

d. **Social Networking** websites are increasingly providing a legitimate gateway to new job opportunities. This is largely driven by the accelerated rate at which recruitment firms are adopting these channels as fast and inexpensive alternatives to sourcing job candidates.

Social networking sites can take the form of social blogs, weblogs, online forums, virtual communities and podcasts. Check out the following:
- www.linkedin.com
- www.twitter.com
- www.facebook.com
- www.myspace.com

Life Story - Maria

I thought I'd try my luck. I logged onto "Seek" to see if there were any legitimate work at home opportunities. There were many "Be Your Own Boss, Earn $1000 per day" type ads that seemed a little far-fetched, but not many genuine job ads.

I tried entering different keywords: "flexible hours", "work at home", "work from home" and then I found it! It looked promising: "Work ten hours per week, research experience preferred, government funded project." I polished up my C.V. and emailed it in response to the ad.

A week later I got a call regarding the job. After a lengthy phone discussion I was invited in for an interview. I was told not to "suit-up" as the company is relaxed on dress code. Phew! The transition from maternity lycra to stiff corporate attire can be so unforgiving!

As soon as I sat down with my prospective employers, they appeared keen to get me on board.

Cont...

www.teleworkingmum.com.au

...Cont

I was later told that the type of candidates that applied were mainly students and travelers. The number of hours per week didn't seem to attract too many job seekers, and the 'work from home' aspect made the job seem somewhat dubious to the serious job seekers.

Far from phony, the job was part of a large national Federal Government research project through a small private company who was contracted to a prestigious Australian university. The project had been running for over five years and had the potential to run for a further five.

I was offered the job and was given the option to join up either as an employee or a sub contractor. The pay rate factored in expenses such as broadband and telephone usage, so was quite generous. Almost five years later I am still with the company and remain happy working from home. Needless to say I am reaping many benefits - including spending valuable time with my toddler and newborn baby - and have not looked back since!

4. Become a freelancer / contractor

Freelancing is a great way to approach re-entering the workforce as a mum. Essentially, to work as a freelancer means that you are self-employed and not committed to an employer. You may work as the need arises or as the work demands. Freelancers can work for one or a handful of clients, therefore, providing them with the comfort of having an 'employer/employee' style working relationship.

Freelancers usually have greater control over role management, and therefore your choice to work from home may be more easily accepted by your clients.

> **'Microjobs' is the term used to describe multiple, small, jobs. These are usually from different employers and often can be on a freelance / contract basis.**

The best way to approach freelancing is to spread the word to all your contacts – both current and past. Make a list of people you have or had a positive working relationship with. Don't just include past managers. Peers could very well provide you with the leads you need to get started on your freelancing journey! Then announce to your group of contacts that you are now available for freelance work. Also ask them to pass on your details to other suitable contacts that they feel may also be appropriate.

If approaching a current or former employer about freelancing, find out what their company policy is on freelance/contract work. Many companies have clauses in their employee contracts prohibiting them from freelancing back to the company after they resign, are retrenched or are on maternity leave, within a certain period, for example six months. After this time lapses you are then free to engage as a contractor or freelancer through the organisation.

Treat your freelance work as a business: promote and market yourself extensively, build a web site, send out newsletters and network as much as possible!

5. Start your own business

Do you have a bright idea about a new product or service, or perhaps you've held a long term desire to branch out on your own? Well, becoming a mum often incites major changes in your career path. Sometimes it's because you've had a break from your usual job and have found the inspiration to follow your dreams. Other times, unfortunately, many mums experience too many barriers to returning to work as an employee and find that becoming your own boss provides a solution to many of your return to work woes. Chapter 11 discusses in more detail the requirements for starting your own business as a mum.

6. Alternative income options

Making money from home is also possible via non-traditional work roles. If you don't want to commit to a regular job or business, then there are other ways of generating money from home. These options don't always offer a guaranteed regular income but if you're looking at earning a few extra dollars every now and then they can certainly help.

Online marketplaces
The internet and technology has added a whole new dimension to our trading marketplaces. Online trading (buying and selling) is now available to anyone with access to a computer and the internet – and with the abundance of internet cafes worldwide, this means virtually anyone can do this.

eBay is one of the most popular online marketplaces, but there are many others that also exist. eBay is reputable and secure but there are still some loopholes. It's best to begin small and work out if it's suitable for you. There are online tutorials and courses you can attend, and your local community center or adult education center may offer courses on this topic. If you're planning on using eBay as a serious means of income it is recommended that you undertake a course or two prior to commencing.

Cottage industry
This is a small-scale industry working from home, and usually on a part-time basis. It usually involves some form of light manufacturing and typically includes items such as household products (e.g. jams, cookies), arts and crafts, clothing, knitting, art, jewellery, toys, candles, aromatherapy products, soaps, linen, manchester, furniture, handbags, stationery, etc. Selling channels for these items include: online trading or auction sites, craft markets, retailers, distributors, online stores etc.

Caution: *You may be liable to pay tax on any income generated via avenues such as cottage industry crafts and online auction sites if your income* *is classified as a business, but not if it is considered a hobby. Check with your tax advisor for more details.*

Life Story - Anna

Anna, a mother of two boys under the age of four first started using eBay to sell her pre-loved baby clothing. She bought good quality clothing for her children and it was a shame to see so many of them outgrown when hardly used.

The baby clothing sold exceptionally well so Anna scoured the rest of her home to get rid of unwanted items and generate an income at the same time. She was so pleased with the return that she expanded her collection by sourcing new items from Sunday markets and garage sales.

On average Anna was earning approximately $800 per month from the profits of her eBay sales. Aside from her occasional treks to the markets or local garage sales, the bulk of her efforts were undertaken in the comfort of her own home, flexibly around her children. On average, Anna dedicated around ten hours of her time every week, yet she was able to take time off when required or increase her efforts when possible.

www.teleworkingmum.com.au

Keywords

When pursuing online job opportunities, the keywords used to undertake your search is important to your search results. If you're looking for telework opportunities it's important to understand the terminology used to reference this work style. For example, the following terms all refer to telework:

- Telework / teleworking
- Telecommute / telecommuting
- Work from home
- Work at home
- eWork
- Cyberwork

The keywords returning the greatest search results in online job advertisements are:

- work from home
- work at home

Beware the scams

Unfortunately, searching for home-based work can often be plagued with scams and illegitimate job postings. Knowing what to look for and what to avoid can make your quest a far more positive – and safer - experience. It can also save you a lot of time, effort and money!

Genuine job opportunities generally offer a specified remuneration for a defined job role. This does not usually require you to part with your money in any way. In other words, a legitimate employer will pay you, without the need for you to pay them.

Questions to ask a prospective employer

1. What duties does my role involve?
2. What will my salary be?
3. Will I be paid a set rate/salary or will it be commission based?
4. What is the pay cycle? (Do I get paid weekly, fortnightly or monthly?)
5. Am I entitled to sick leave, maternity leave, annual leave, etc?

As a general rule, jobs or businesses offering an upfront investment (usually money) are often scams. Obviously if you are looking at buying a business you may need to invest money before you can start operating; however, you will need to research this thoroughly before committing. Check with your state and federal government business agencies to research a business if you are considering buying it or taking out a franchise.

Some genuine telework job opportunities require you to be set up as a contractor/freelancer. This might require you to provide and utilise your own equipment such as telephone, fax, computer, general business software, etc. Being asked to invest in non-generic equipment or software – particularly if the cost is significant – may be worth investigating further with your future employer as well as your state government watchdog.

Warning!

Beware if faced with any of the following scenarios.

1. Job requires you to invest in or hand over your money.
2. Job requires you to purchase software, equipment or materials that are non-generic business/work tools.
3. Advertised job or business offers a high income with minimal skills or effort to undertake the work.

Either avoid these situations altogether, or investigate further by checking with government bodies providing a watchdog role for jobs and / or businesses.

Official anti-scam websites

The following Australian Government websites may assist if you want to investigate a possible scam. They also provide assistance if you have fallen victim to an employment or business scam.

- www.scamwatch.gov.au
- www.fido.asic.gov.au FIDO – Australian Securities and Investment Commission. Provides listing of types of scams and warnings issued, particularly for financial products and services.
- www.accc.gov.au (Australian Competition and Consumer Commission)

Chapter 8

Telework Action Plan

By this stage you have been tempted by the benefits, considered the limitations and developed a keen motivation to achieving your telework goals. Now it's time to roll up your sleeves and get stuck into the hands-on process of formulating your plan and drafting your proposal.

Define your objectives

The first step is to clearly define your objectives. This means you need to decide what it is you want: i.e., are you seeking reduced hours (e.g., part-time), telework, flex-time or a combination of these or other flexible work options? Once this has been established, you need to focus on specifics. For instance, if you want to work from home do you propose to undertake your entire job from home or parts of it?

When drafting your objectives be hopeful yet realistic - i.e., is your plan achievable within your employer's and your own agenda? Be clear and concise about what you want and then document it.

Remember, you may not get precisely what you want, although it's worth putting a stake in the ground as a starting point, and negotiating your way from there.

Preparing your telework proposal

> Around three quarters of employee requests for flexibility are approved by employers in Australia.
> One in ten are declined.
>
> *Source: The Australian Work Life Index 2009.*

Research

Does your employer have a policy on flexible working arrangements, or more specifically, teleworking? Find out and review the relevant information.

Check out the company's website or intranet for initial information, then contact your Human Resources representative or department if you require further information. Also, read any employee handbooks you were given when you commenced work with the company if you are approaching your current employer.

If there is no formal telework program in place, look for any reference to other flexible work options such as 'flextime' (flexible start/finish times), 'job share', etc. The degree to which a company provides other flexible working arrangements is a good indicator as to how your proposal for telework might be received.

Speak with others who have negotiated similar arrangements with your employer, to gain an insight on the process and likelihood of acceptance.

If you can't locate any relevant information, research the company's competitors or key clients to see if they have introduced telework into their organisation and to what extent. This information can provide a good incentive for your employer to consider your proposal.

Breaking the news

It's a good idea to speak with your employer initially to briefly let them know of your plan. Book a time to meet with him/her at a later date to discuss your proposal in detail. This will give your employer a 'heads-up' on what to expect, allowing them to also come in prepared. If necessary book a meeting room so that your employer is not distracted by other issues (phone calls or other people) and so that your discussion remains confidential and fully focused.

Staying positive

When discussing your proposal remain positive and optimistic. Approach your employer as an ally – not an adversary. Focus on the benefits your proposal will bring to the company and if you foresee issues arising from your proposed changes, be prepared to offer solutions.

If you are asked about anything which you cannot immediately provide a response to, let your employer know that you would like more time to consider this and follow up on it at a later date.

Whilst you are requesting flexibility from your employer, remember that flexibility on your part is also necessary. If there are aspects of your proposal that do not fit your employer's requirements, you may either need to re-work your plan or forgo certain parts of it.

Written proposal and oral presentation

A well researched and prepared proposal is essential. Rather than emailing this or handing over a copy to your manager, make sure you arrange a time, in confidence, to present this verbally to him/her in person. Have two printed copies on hand during your presentation: one for you to help guide you through your oral presentation, and the other to give to your manager.

The document provides your manager the opportunity to review aspects of your plan in more detail, with a more informed consideration. It also provides the information when necessary to relay your proposal to more senior management if necessary.

Hint: *When arranging a time for your presentation to your manager, mention briefly what you intend to discuss. Don't spring up the issue unexpectedly in your meeting. Allow your manager the opportunity to consider his/her standpoint before you present yours.*

Explain why you want to telework
- Don't waffle! Provide a short, sharp reason for your request to telework.
- Focus on the benefits of teleworking for your employer.

- Reinforce your value to the company and how teleworking will improve your productivity, efficiency, improve your wellbeing, reduce stress, commute times, etc.
- Draw examples of how some of your major achievements in the past may have been accomplished via some degree of telework (or, if you did indeed telework to complete tasks in the past, highlight these).

Promote yourself

Assess your personal attributes, firstly to see if are you cut out for telework, but secondly to pitch yourself as a strong candidate for telework. Here are some noteworthy attributes which you could highlight in your proposal:

- Self-starter
- Proven performer
- Self-disciplined
- Well organized
- Highly motivated
- Good time-manager
- Work independently

Be sure to include succinct examples of how you have successfully demonstrated these attributes in your role. Further details you might consider including in your telework proposal are constructive responses to the following questions:

- **How are you an asset to the company?**
- **What value do you contribute to your team, department or business unit?**

- What is your unique selling point - which sets you apart from other employees?

Your role / job function

Consider the following questions and provide clear, concise answers:
- How is your role suited to telework?
- What aspects of your role will flourish?
- What aspects of your role are best performed 'at work' as opposed to 'at home'?

Dissect your job by function

Indicate which of your job functions can be done from home and those which need to be performed at your employer's or client's site. Depending on your role, you may find that all of your job can be successfully undertaken from home. Here is an example of a Marketing Assistant's job, with each function itemised:

1. Take minutes for weekly marketing meeting. *(From home via teleconference/skype)*
2. Prepare monthly sales charts. *(home)*
3. Produce client profiles. *(attend client site for research material and interviews then complete profiles at home)*
4. Update corporate website content. *(home)*
5. Bi-annual sales team strategy conference. *(attend conference site)*

Gaps and obstacles

Consider any gaps or obstacles to your role which may arise out of your changed working arrangement. Ensure you address these in your proposal, offering practical and achievable solutions or a work-around.

Your schedule and availability

Provide a basic outline with the following details:
- Which days/hours will you telework?
- What times/hours will you be available:
  - For work?
  - For contacting?
- How can you be contacted? Phone, fax, email, Instant Messaging, SMS, Skype, other?
- State whether or not you will be available for on-site meetings or provide alternatives (e.g., teleconference)

Communication / Collaboration

Discuss how you will communicate and collaborate with all major stakeholders of your role. How will you communicate with:
- **Your manager?**
- **Your colleagues?**
- **Your clients?**
- **Your suppliers?**
- **Other relevant stakeholders?**

Describe your workspace

Some employers are keen to have their employees work from home, given the vast benefits teleworking offers. However, some of these employers have strict requirements for the home-based workspaces of their teleworking employees.

For example, one employer requires a physical assessment of the home setup prior to initiating a telework arrangement. This employer requires that the workspace must be in a separate room which is utilised solely for work purposes. Another employer stipulates no television, radio or other forms of audio/visual entertainment can be seen or heard from the employee's work area during work times. Obviously this is to minimise distractions, and to also provide a professional setting in case the teleworker engages in telephone contact with clients or suppliers.

When preparing your proposal, consider the following questions regarding your proposed home-based workspace:

- **Is it a dedicated room?**
- **If not, what other uses does this room share (e.g., lounge room)?**
- **Is your workspace free from distractions?**
- **Is your workspace occupational health and safety (OHS) compliant? Undertake a basic risk assessment for OHS.**
   (You might need to refer to your original employee agreement or consult with your OHS or Human Resources representative for assistance.)

Equipment

When teleworking, it is common for employee and employer to share the provision of some of the equipment required or costs incurred to support your work at home.

- What equipment do you require?
- What equipment can you provide?
- What equipment will your employer need to provide?

Security

Providing measures to minimise security threats is an important aspect to cover in your telework proposal. Security is a serious issue of concern for many employers when it comes to telework.

Consider the security issues surrounding your job. Perhaps you deal with sensitive employee records or legal documents. If this is the case, consider how you will store, retrieve and discard these documents safely and securely.

Many businesses have formal processes to ensure an optimum level of security is maintained. Outline the ones relevant to your role and explain how you plan to comply with these requirements once you start working from home.

Personal issues

Given that your employer is most likely aware of your caring responsibilities, you need to explain how this will fit in with your proposed work routine. For example, if you have a baby, here is an outline of how you might pitch it to your employer:

- I will undertake two hours' work from 4-6 pm while my partner is available to baby-sit, or,
- a family member is available for babysitting during my designated work times, or,
- my child is in day care, or
- I will work two hours per day, flexibly, usually around my child's nap times, for example, 9-10am and then 2-3pm.

Hint: *Working minimal hours to begin with, e.g., up to two or three hours per day, will provide a more realistic basis to work flexibly around your family. Longer hours are less amenable to flexibility and need a more rigid routine as well as a reliable source of child care.*

Propose a trial period

Include a clause in your proposal for a short trial period, for example, three months. This provides an opportunity to review the arrangement and make any changes if required. This offers both your employer and you an exit strategy if the arrangement is not working to the benefit of both parties.

Research and facts

Now that you are clear on what it is that you want to propose to your employer, you need to develop a convincing argument to hook your employer's interest in your plan. The best way to do this is to use hard sell tactics: hit them with persuasive examples of potential cost savings for their business. As the saying goes *"money talks"*, and in business this couldn't be more apt!

To do so you will need to draw in some of the data from Chapter 3 (see section on 'Business Benefits') to outline the potential cost benefits to your employer. These figures are based on current research by leading private and government organisations in Australia and around the world. Include statistics, research, case-studies and good examples of success stories demonstrating the benefits of telework for employers.

In addition to financial savings, employers are interested in increased productivity, lowering costs and improving efficiencies. A lot of this information is available throughout this book.

For a sample telework proposal template visit:
www.teleworkingmum.com.au

Further to this, the Telework Australia website maintains useful information that you could also draw on to include in your proposal. For more information visit:

www.teleworkaustralia.com.au

What if your employer says NO?

Whether or not you are granted your wish to telework is generally at your manager/employer's discretion. This decision is usually based on whether they believe there is a business fit or need to do so. Furthermore, if your proposed changes to your existing role would likely cause excessive disruption, cost or transformation to your employer's business, then this would be seen as reasonable grounds for rejection.

Preparing a proposal that is supported by persuasive facts and examples of how telework can benefit the business provides more ammunition in persuading your employer to agree to your plan. However, if you are faced with rejection, remind yourself that not all decisions are final. If you are game enough to tackle some common employer concerns you may be able to successfully turn a negative outcome into a positive one.

However, before you go down that track you first need to request a written explanation from your employer detailing why your proposal was rejected. (If you are eligible under the Fair Work Act to make a request for flexibility, your employer must provide you with a written response to your proposal within 21 days. Refer Chapter 5 for more details.) There should be some scope for you to address your employer's reasons for rejecting your proposal. Following are some common employer concerns and some suggested responses which you can arm yourself with:

Some common employer objections and how to respond to them

Objection 1 - You will lose touch with your colleagues / managers / clients.

Response Examples:

1. I will be available via regular teleconferences / email / instant messaging / 'at work' meetings.
2. I will be available to attend the office when necessary.

3. Research indicates that teleworkers are generally more available for meetings than 'at work' employees.
4. I will attend the workplace every Wednesday to maintain regular contact with my peers and managers.

Objection 2 - Teleworking will cost too much to implement and / or maintain.

Response Examples:

1. I have my own computer and am willing to pay 50% of the cost of high speed internet.
2. The increase in productivity for your business could be as high as 40%.
3. Research indicates that teleworking potentially saves employers around $10,000 each year by reducing absenteeism and job retention costs.
4. The savings in overheads (such as office space, utilities expenses, etc) usually outweigh the costs required to initiate and support telework.

Objection 3 - It's unfair to the rest of the team who are not offered telework or other flexible work options.

Response Examples:

1. I understand that Telework is not suitable for everyone or every role. Perhaps you should look at introducing new work alternatives for employees who need to perform their role at work, for example, flexible start and finish times, compressed working week, or 48/52 extended leave options.

2. Teleworking would considerably improve my ability to manage my job in addition to my primary care responsibilities. This would be a temporary arrangement for the next eighteen months until my child commences school. I am happy to undertake a short trial period to demonstrate to you my commitment and ability to perform to similar or better standards under this new arrangement.
3. My role is uniquely suited to telework as it bears considerable autonomy and extensive internet research, with little customer interaction. This lends itself well to a home-based working environment.

Objection 4 - It will be difficult to monitor your work.

Response Examples:

1. I plan to draft a telework arrangement which will include a set of well-defined deliverables, against which my performance can be closely monitored and measured.
2. I will provide a weekly status report to my manager, outlining completed and planned tasks.

Objection 5 - It's inconvenient for customers.

Response Examples:

1. I will be available via the usual channels (telephone and email) for customer enquiries, during set business hours.
2. Customers will contact me via the head office switchboard and their calls can be routed to my

mobile phone. Alternatively, customers can call me direct.

3. I will install a dedicated home-office telephone line which will be utilised exclusively for business calls.

If you are still finding it hard to persuade your employer, try a different approach. For example:

- If you have proposed a full telework arrangement, re-approach your manager/employer with fewer teleworking days, incorporating an 'at work' component as well.

- Offer to complete a small project from home outside of normal work hours to prove your commitment and ability to telework.

- Suggest to initially telework on a casual basis, for appropriate tasks. This will aid in proving your suitability for telework, and will also give your employer more time to adjust to the arrangement.

If you still have no luck it's time to face the facts and ask yourself:

a. Is it worth moving into a more flexible profession or role?

b. Is it time to find a new employer?

Caution: *If your telework proposal is accepted by your immediate manager, be sure to obtain agreement from all other relevant parties to ensure your plans won't be intercepted further down the line!*

Life Story - Brian & Pietra

When Brian and Pietra became parents, the thought of living off one income caused much apprehension for the couple, particularly as Pietra was the family breadwinner. After several discussions the couple decided that Pietra would return to work full-time after six months' maternity leave at which point Brian would take on the primary care role for their daughter as well as continue his job as a healthcare administrator on a part-time basis.

Brian negotiated a flexible work plan with his employer by reducing his hours to three days a week, two of which were based at home. His core job functions are highly suited to telework and involve database management, data entry and reporting, which can be undertaken flexibly, regardless of location.

He finds it very rewarding to be involved in the day to day rearing of their baby girl and his schedule is flexible enough to enable him to attend to appointments such as the maternal health nurse visits for his daughter.

www.teleworkingmum.com.au

Developing a telework agreement

Once your telework proposal has gained approval and you have secured consent from all relevant parties, it is time to start developing a telework agreement. A telework agreement is the formal process of documenting your agreed work plan.

An agreement is recommended in any telework or other flexible working arrangement. The agreement must clearly outline the responsibilities of the employee as well as the employer. This agreement should be mutually accepted by the employee and the employer and reviewed for applicability at no later than three months from implementation. Subsequent reviews should be scheduled regularly at a time period no longer than twelve months apart.

Your proposal is a good starting point for developing your agreement. Most points in your proposal would have already been discussed with your manager, therefore you would know if any items need to be modified, which are to be included and which are to be omitted.

Following is a basic checklist of issues and questions to cover when developing your teleworking agreement. It should be expanded further by incorporating the relevant items from your proposal.

Agreement basics

Whilst it seems obvious, you would be surprised at how many agreements and other formal documents fail to provide basic information outlining:

a. Who – Who is the agreement between? Specify your full name and your employer's business name.

b. What – What is the purpose of the agreement?

c. When – What date will the agreement take effect? Also, if your agreement is for a specified period only (e.g., 12 months) you should also specify the end date.

Statement of flexible working arrangements

A short paragraph succinctly describing your agreed flexible working arrangements should form the introduction to your telework and/or flexible working agreement. Optional information to include here would be the purpose of your flexible working arrangement, expected frequency and duration.

Schedule & availability

- Agreed number of hours to be worked by employee per day/per week/per month.

- Will these hours need to be done during set times, or can they be worked flexibly? If you elect set times these need to be stated in the agreement, e.g., Mondays 10am-2pm.

- What times will you be available for contact via telephone and / or email?

Communication / Collaboration

- How will you communicate with staff and/or customers? For example, telephone, email, fax, teleconference, videoconference, instant messaging, etc.
- Outline how you will participate in meetings.

Equipment

- What equipment do you require to undertake your role from home, e.g., computer, fax, internet connection, software, etc?
- Who will purchase/supply the equipment required?
- Who will own the equipment supplied?
- Who will be responsible for the maintenance and related costs of equipment?
- Who will be responsible for the insurance of equipment?

Outline accountability and define performance measures

This point is critical as it defines your goals and sets expectations. A performance review for teleworkers should be largely based on measurable achievements, as opposed to attendance or hours worked. Therefore it is essential to document your work goals and provide details of how each achievement will be measured. This should be done before you set out on your teleworking journey and of course, it should be undertaken in consultation with your employer, with both parties agreeing to each objective and its associated measure(s).

For example:

Objective 1: Complete 2 customer profiles each week.
Measures / Deliverables:
1. Each completed customer profile must contain accurate, current information.
2. The data required for each customer profile is per the marketing department template, consisting of: customer name, revenue, market position, media coverage, competitor analysis and product/service offerings.

Objective 2: Update corporate website information.
Measures / Deliverables:
1. Update website at least once a week with the following information: media releases and team news.
2. Update website at least once a month with the following information: corporate collateral, monthly newsletter and company announcements.

In these examples the employee assumes full accountability for each objective. Where there is an overlap of roles or responsibilities, these should be documented mapping out who is accountable for which deliverable.

Another aspect to incorporate in this section is a clear indication of which tasks will be undertaken at your employer's premises and which will be undertaken from home. If you intend to perform your entire job at home then this needs to be stated as well.

Hint: *It might be helpful to document your achievements and email them to your manager at the end of each week or month. Alternatively you may wish to schedule regular meetings with your manager – whether via telephone or in person – to discuss your progress.*

Expenses

- What expenses will be reimbursed by your employer (e.g., telephone calls, internet subscription, etc)?
- What are the procedures for claiming expenses via your employer? (This might be already covered in your original employee agreement/contract.)
- What expenses will you cover?

Employee entitlements

- Refer back to the standard employee terms and conditions included in your original employee contract. If you don't have one you will need to add these details into your telework agreement.
- Access to training and development opportunities: teleworkers should maintain the same level of access to training and development as their non-teleworking colleagues.

Workspace

- Explain any specific workspace requirements and how you will provide or maintain these.

Occupational health and safety

- How will Occupational Health and Safety compliance be achieved? Note any specific areas of concern and address how you will manage these.

Security

- Document any security requirements for your work-related data, equipment, materials, documents, etc.
- Explain how you will maintain processes in line with your employer's security policies.

Personal issues

- Provide details of suitable childcare arrangements whilst you undertake your work, or an explanation of how you will manage this.

Review and exit

- Define a process for reviewing or ending the agreement. An initial period of three months for a first review works well for many people. Perhaps a second review might be six months later and then annually after that. If things are not working out either for you or your employer, an exit strategy allows you to rescind the agreement if or when necessary.

Approval

Obtain formal approval of your agreement by having the appropriate managers sign your agreement. They should also write their full name, position/title and date of approval.

www.teleworkingmum.com.au

FAQs

Do I need a telework agreement?

It is strongly advisable to develop a telework agreement with your employer if you intend to undertake telework on a regular or ongoing basis. This provides a written consensus on how and when you undertake your work from home and also provides details of what your expected deliverables are.

Who prepares the telework agreement?

Firstly, speak with your employer to find out if they already have a process for drafting agreements of this kind. Also, find out if your employer has a telework or flexible work policy. If so, you can use this as a guide, modifying relevant details as they specifically apply to you.

Some organisations have their own human resources specialists who are usually experienced at drafting workplace agreements. You can then review this and add any further information you think is relevant so that your agreed working conditions are comprehensively covered.

If your workplace doesn't have a policy in place and also doesn't have the resources to produce your telework or flexible work agreement, you can do this yourself using the information and guidelines provided in this chapter. Be sure to have your employer/manager review and sign this. Also keep an original signed agreement for your own records.

A sample telework agreement is available at www.teleworkingmum.com.au

Teleworking tips for employers

- If adopting a flexible work-model this should be promoted and made available to all levels of the organisation, if possible.

- Gender assumptions should be erased. Don't assume men don't want access to flexible modes of working; likewise, don't assume that women with children aren't looking for career advancement.

- Maintain open channels of communication with your staff. Schedule regular staff consultations to gauge their satisfaction with current / planned work models. Can improvements be made to help them achieve their desired level of work / life balance?

- Review all new or vacant roles for their suitability to various 'flexible' work models, e.g., can a work at home or compressed hours component be offered to applicants? Use this as a selling tool for these positions to attract the best talent for your business.

- Include all staff in relevant meetings and don't exclude those working flexibly. Perhaps offer flexible modes of delivery such as teleconference to ensure you include those working from home.

- Opportunities for training and development should be equally available to all staff, regardless of whether they work flexibly, full-time or part-time.

- Opportunities for promotion should be based on merit and equally available to all employees.

- Encourage parents to return to work from parental leave. Keep in contact with employees on parental leave and keep them informed of relevant business updates. Offer them small pieces of work they can complete at home, at flexible times.

Useful References

- For a sample telework proposal and flexible work agreement visit www.teleworkingmum.com.au

Chapter 9

Family Friendly Workplaces

What do they offer?

A 'Family-Friendly' workplace is one which offers its employees genuine work/life balance through various flexible work options. Family-friendly employers may also offer programs that support families making the transition back into the workforce as new parents. Examples of the kinds of support or programs available by recognised 'family-friendly' workplaces include:

- Extended paid maternity / parental leave
- Extended unpaid maternity / parental leave
- Breast feeding rooms or facilities in the workplace
- Parents' rooms
- 'Keep in touch' programs for parents on parental leave
- Support with child care either as a service in or near the workplace, and / or subsidised fees
- Provision of free car parking during parental leave
- Having special family days such as bring your child to work day, or family picnic day, etc.
- Job share
- Part-time work
- Compressed hours (working longer hours to shorten the working week)
- Flexible start and finish times

- Telework (work from home)
- Using 'make-up' time for staff to make up work time if they use work hours to attend appointments
- Arrangements for sabbatical leave
- Extended annual or other leave options (e.g., leave without pay)

The need for family friendly workplaces

The underlying feature of a family friendly workplace is flexibility. Flexibility in the workforce is increasingly in demand due to some of the following dynamics:

1. A growing percentage of working women with parental caring responsibilities (around 69% of working mums have dependent children).[9]

2. Australia's ageing population is on the rise, and more women are bearing children later in life, which can often lead to a dual caring role.[10] This places significant barriers to managing work and caring responsibilities.

3. The rise in single parent families. Single parent families represent almost one quarter of all families with dependent children in Australia.[11]

---

[9] Human Rights Equal Opportunity Commission (HREOC), *Striking the balance: women, men, work and family discussion paper*, 2005 and ABS, *Labor Force* electronic delivery, 2008

[10] Carers are most likely to be within the 35-55 year age range. Source: ABS, 2008.

[11] ABS, *Census of Population and Housing: Selected Social and Housing Characteristics, Australia, 2006*.

What do employers gain?

There are considerable incentives for employer organisations who offer family friendly programs. Most of these are similar to the list of benefits outlined in Chapter 2 – Business Benefits. As a re-cap, some of these include:

- Increased cost savings
- Greater productivity
- Improved branding and reputation as employer of choice
- Improvements in business efficiencies
- Lower overhead costs
- Employee satisfaction
- Employee loyalty
- Reduced absenteeism
- Lower attrition rates
- …and much more!

Who are they?

There are an increasing number of government and industry awards which provide public recognition of employers who demonstrate excellence in work/life balance. These awards publicise details of the innovative ways in which organisations offer flexible programs and other initiatives to support working families.

The National Work-Life Balance Awards provides a list of finalists demonstrating genuine flexible working arrangements and a commitment to continuous improvements in work/life balance programs within their workplaces. There are also various other awards at a state or national level which provide formal recognition of an employer's flexible policies, practices or initiatives.

The Equal Opportunity for Women in the Workplace Agency (EOWA) is another Australian Government body providing excellent leadership and support for employers to provide better outcomes for women in the workplace. EOWA conducts the annual 'Employer of Choice for Women' Awards. For more information visit: www.eowa.gov.au.

Based on former finalists of the various government and industry awards, the following list provides an example of some of the employers offering telework, together with other flexible programs.

- Alcoa Australia Limited
- ANZ Bank
- Aurora Energy
- Australian Federal Police
- Deakin University
- Grampians Community Health Centre
- Greenslopes Private Hospital
- Hydro Tasmania
- IBM
- John Wiley & Sons Australia
- La Trobe University
- Minter Ellison
- Mercy Health
- Microsoft Australia
- Monash University
- National Australia Bank

- Nortel
- NSW National Parks and Wildlife Service
- NSW Road Traffic Authority
- Queensland Rail
- Sara Lee Household and Body Care
- SC Johnson
- Shell Australia
- Sydney Water Corporation
- Telstra
- The University of Melbourne
- Toshiba
- University of Western Australia
- Westpac Banking Corporation

The way of the future

It is evident that teleworking and other forms of flexible work styles are sought not just by working parents, but the broader workforce in general. Aside from family responsibilities, other life situations can sometimes call for greater flexibility at work and include reasons such as: change in caring responsibilities, personal wellbeing issues, interest in furthering one's education, desire to devote more time to personal interests (such as hobbies), desire to travel, and many others. As such, flexibility at work is now emerging as a highly prized incentive for employees, which is driving employers to change the ways in which they manage and engage their workforce.

The business magazine BRW released results of their survey in 2010 of Australia's best workplaces. Flexibility was rated the highest desired job asset, followed by a culture of trust and other bonuses. Flexibility requires a shift in management attitude towards a results-driven environment. This modern sentiment supports getting the work done well, regardless of the location or when it is performed. Some of the benefits offered by the winning workplaces include:

- Flexible start and finish times
- Work from home options
- Educational benefits
- Health Insurance
- Gymnasium memberships
- Additional maternity benefits
- Chill-out rooms at work
- Access to entertainment at work (such as Wiis, Xboxes, iPads, etc).

It is interesting to note some of the attributes common amongst many businesses on the winner's list:

1. Young businesses that had not been entrenched in old ways

2. In the Information Technology professional services field (almost half of companies that made the list are within this segment)

3. Medium-sized enterprises.

Useful References

➢ EOWA Employer of Choice for Women. The Equal Opportunity for Women in Australia lists employers in Australia providing outstanding opportunities for women in the workforce. http://www.eowa.gov.au

➢ National Work–Life Balance Awards, and also Fresh Ideas for Work and Family (Australian Government grants to support the implementation of work/family balance for small businesses). http://www.deewr.gov.au

➢ Breastfeeding friendly workplaces. http://www.breastfeedingfriendly.com.au

➢ Victorian Government – Ways to Work business site. (Includes the Fair and Flexible Employer Awards.) http://ways2work.business.vic.gov.au

Chapter 10

Work at Home Essentials

Planning to work from home can be very exciting; from preparing your new work area, to contemplating your new lifestyle, it can all be fun and enlivening! However, there are many issues that need to be considered before embarking on your home-based work to ensure your plans are not only smoothly and positively achieved, but also sustained.

Initially, most people tend to focus on the tangible aspects of setting up from home, (such as tools, technology, furniture and equipment). These are the more immediate, and somewhat more obvious, aspects of your telework action plan.

However, teleworking involves consideration and compliance with a range of laws and regulations that apply to the home-based worker. Some of these are regulated by your local council and others are an extension of your employer's legal obligations. If you are embarking on a new home-based business, you also need to research your legal and taxation obligations.

This chapter provides a practical approach to preparing the groundwork for your initiation into telework. It discusses the essentials and also helps you draw a more realistic picture about what you need and what you can do without when first establishing your workspace and routine at home. It also covers vital information about council regulations, permits and registrations as well as legal requirements.

What will you need?

When ascertaining what you will need to support your work from home plan, you need to factor in both the major items such as equipment, technology, etc., as well as any incidental items such as stationery. These items might seem insignificant but can add up to a decent sum if you need regular supplies at hand, so they simply can't be taken for granted!

Your first step is to document everything you will need to facilitate your home-based work. Every item should be listed – yes, even paper clips and pens! This exercise will help you obtain a clear perspective on the total cost of establishing your telework initiative.

It is important to keep any receipts for work-related expenses you incur so that you are able to recover some or all of these costs via:
- your employer through the company's expense claim procedures, or
- the tax system, against your personal or business tax return

A work-related expense can generally be claimed from either your employer or the taxation system, but not both. If you intend to claim from your employer you need to have discussed and mutually agreed to what can be claimed, in advance to incurring the expense.

> ## Life Story
>
> Kate became a freelancer after giving birth to her first child. She obtained a twelve month contract and negotiated to work from home. In many ways Kate was treated like an employee, although her legal setup was as a small business owner. Kate was able to provide some equipment to undertake her work from home, although she negotiated a number of reimbursements from her 'employer' to cover some costs as well.
>
> Kate's hourly rate factored in the following costs:
> - Base rate of pay
> - Superannuation contribution
> - Allowance for local telephone calls
> - Allowance for the full cost of broadband
>
> Kate provided her own notebook computer, printer and telephone. She was responsible for all costs associated with the use and maintenance of this equipment. Kate also provided basic business software such as email and word processing. Her employer provided any work-specific software that was required for Kate to undertake her job.

www.teleworkingmum.com.au

The next step is to consider who will supply these items, or who will cover the cost of these items – you or your employer? Also, who will be responsible for replacing these items if your supply runs out or if the item is damaged? Complete the following checklist, adding any extra items as required.

Checklist - equipment, supplies & technology

Required ✓	Item	Who will supply?	Comments
Supplies			
	A4 paper		
	Pens		
	Envelopes		
	Stapler		
	Hole punch		
	Writing pads		
	Post it notes		
	Paper clips		
	Other		
Equipment			
	Desk		
	Chair		
	Paper shredder		
	Calculator		
	Special lighting		
	Other		
Technology			
	Computer		
	Fax		
	Telephone line		
	Mobile phone		
	Internet connection		
	Software		
	Telephone headset		
	Email		
	Other		

Insurance

Some home insurance policies require you to inform your insurer when you undertake your work or business from home on a permanent or regular basis. It's a good idea to talk to your insurer to discuss what options you have for insuring any additional items of value you have in your home relating to your work, but also to check if your current home or contents policy is affected by the change in your circumstances.

The 'checklist' table is a good place to start to pinpoint which items remain the property of your employer, and which are yours. Your employer should have insurance for items that are owned by them, but it is definitely in your best interests to draft an inventory of items, outlining ownership and insurance responsibilities. This inventory can also be included in your telework agreement prior to signoff.

An inventory can be as simple as this:

Item	Supplied/ owned by	Asset Number	Insured by owner?
Desk	Employee	D100	Yes
Notebook	Employer	TR210z4	Yes
Fax	Employer	TZ8UJL2	Yes

Technology and communications

The teleworking mum usually requires some form of technology and communications to enable her to communicate or collaborate with her employer, colleagues and/or customers. There are many forms of telecommunications accessible to the home worker. Your requirements may vary depending on the nature of your job.

Typical technology for the teleworking mum may include some or all of the following:

1. **Telephone**
2. **Internet access (preferably high speed broadband or wireless)**
3. **Email system**
4. **Computer**
5. **Fax**
6. **Instant messaging**
7. **PC Camera (for videoconferencing)**

Internet

The internet is a significant enabler of telework. It provides access to data, files, systems and technology for teleworkers to undertake their work. Having access to high speed broadband allows a faster means to download, upload, process and access data and systems, therefore making life as a home based worker far more productive.

To view and compare internet / broadband service providers and what they have to offer, visit:

www.whirlpool.net.au

Wireless connectivity

Mobile phones and notebook computers allow teleworkers the convenience of mobility. Whilst you might work primarily from home, and possibly in a dedicated space within your home, the ease of transporting your work to any location provides greater scope for managing your busy schedule, together with the demands of your family.

Wireless broadband and the declining cost to access this technology is providing increasing adoption by users worldwide. Furthermore, it is sometimes cheaper and easier to opt for this type of connectivity, compared with a fixed line contract. The reliability of this technology in rural areas is also rapidly improving, offering greater incentive for users to embrace this option.

Voice over internet protocol (VoiP)

VoiP transmits voice communications over IP networks. An example is where telephone calls are made using the internet. Other terms used to refer to this technology include: broadband telephony, internet telephony and voice over broadband.

Costs are quite low compared to standard land line calls, which make this technology too good to ignored by teleworkers.

To make VoiP calls you will need the following:

1. Broadband internet connection

2. VoiP phone (either hardware or software based) – this is a handset which may look like an ordinary phone but plugs into your computer or broadband router/hub. The alternative is to use your own phone and purchase an analogue phone adaptor to allow you to utilise this for VoiP services as well as your standard telephone service.

3. A VoiP service provider – you will most likely need to subscribe to a plan like you do with your standard telephone service provider. There are many service providers offering VoiP services, check out the following site which provides a summary of the many services available to Australian based customers:

www.voipchoice.com.au

If you are working as an employee, find out what your technology and communications requirements are and then negotiate with your employer to determine which of these they are prepared to pay for. For example, you may already have a telephone connection in your home, but perhaps your employer may want you to have a separate, dedicated line which is used exclusively for work. Find out if they are willing to cover the cost of the installation, monthly plan fees as well as the cost of calls. This would be the ideal scenario. Some employers increase hourly rates of pay to incorporate a base amount for these expenses (for employees or contractors); otherwise they can opt to pay for individual expense items.

Keep a record of all work-related calls or other telecommunications expenses you outlay so that you can claim these at the end of the financial year. Consult with your accountant for specific advice on eligibility.

A productive work area

The successful teleworking mum creates a workspace in her home that is organised, comfortable and well equipped.

The ideal workspace would be a dedicated room, set up with all your requirements to facilitate an optimum working environment: desk, computer, internet access, ergonomic chair, bookshelves, filing system, or whatever furniture or equipment you need to get your work done. By having your own room you could simply close the door to delineate the work/home boundaries. This would also be the best setup to attract a greater proportion of expense claims through the taxation system, saving a considerable amount of money.

However, this is not always possible or practical. Therefore if your work area needs to be part of another room, e.g., living room, ensure that you allow enough space to work comfortably. Being crammed and untidy doesn't foster the best working environment, so keep files or things you don't need for the current project stored in storage boxes in another room or the garage. This may help ease any space issues and it will declutter your area so that you can be more organised, and thus more productive.

Some employers who have work-at-home policies require that teleworkers have a dedicated space to perform their work, and some employers even include a clause stating that this must not be done in front of the television - obviously to minimise distractions. I fully support both of these directives as concentration on any job is crucial and having a dedicated area – not necessarily a dedicated room – adds a degree of legitimacy and continuity to your home based work, giving it an official place in your home.

The flexibility offered through mobile technology, such as notebook computing and wireless broadband, have their benefits which could certainly enhance your work-at-home experience. However, this doesn't mean you can't dedicate a regular place of work within your home and know that this is your reserved space to work from when you need to.

Who should pay for what?

Having some or all of your equipment/tools supplied or subsidised depends on your employer and their willingness to fully support your work at home plan. This also varies, according to your employment situation: are you an employee, freelancer, consultant/contractor or self employed?

For employees, generally most specific work related equipment and tools are supplied by the employer. These can include a computer/laptop, software and telephone. Items such as office furniture, furnishings and some stationery are generally supplied by the employee. Many teleworkers share the cost of internet access with their employer.

If your employer has outlaid expenses in their workplace for you and are unable to make use of them for other employees, then they may not be willing to contribute to your home office set up costs. However, if they are short on space and infrastructure, your proposed work from home arrangements may benefit them as they are essentially using your home as an extension of their workspace. In this case, try to negotiate as much as possible in terms of equipment and set up costs.

When negotiating your work-at-home proposal with your employer be sure to state any equipment you may already have at home which you are prepared to utilise for your work, e.g, computer, fax, email, internet access, desk, etc.

Legal requirements

When you undertake your work from home, regardless of whether it is done on a part-time, casual or permanent basis, there are numerous legal obligations that need to be met.

Council restrictions

Adhering to your local council's regulations is essential. Each local council provides its own set of rules and restrictions pertaining to undertaking your work or business from home. Many of these are standard across many councils, however, there are also some specific regulations that apply to individual councils.

Generally, council laws affecting the home-based worker exist to protect the peace and wellbeing of the community. These laws are usually in force to control noise levels, pollution, traffic/disruptions, hazardous emissions/waste, etc.

The list below is a summary of several common council by-laws which affect the home based worker, including businesses operating at home. To find out which ones apply to you check out your local council's website or give them a call to discuss your teleworking plans.

- Limit to the number of employees working in your home. Usually this is one at any one time, however you may be able to apply for a permit to allow more.
- Your home-based business must be run by a permanent member of your household.
- The business must be operated from within an enclosure – usually your home, garage or granny flat.
- The total area of your business or work operations must not exceed 50 sqm. You may be able to apply for a permit to increase this to 100 sqm, depending on your council. Some councils allow up to one third of your total property size. Check with your council if area coverage is an issue.
- No signage can be displayed which is visible from outside your property.
- Your work or business should not in any way affect your neighbours: noise levels, street parking, traffic flow, etc.
- Utilities usage should not surpass the average domestic usage rates. This includes gas, water and electricity.
- Only one client waiting at any given time.
- Only one delivery / courier visit per day.
- No use of harzardous chemicals or waste.
- In general, these regulations are in place to protect your neighbourhood from being disrupted. People live in

areas zoned as 'residential' and these should not be affected by businesses or workers operating from home.

Permits & registrations

You should check with your local council to see if your type of work or business requires any special permits or registrations in order for you to undertake this from home. Generally, any work involving food or health may require a permit or registration with your local council. It's always best to be on the safe side and enquire first.

Occupational Health and Safety (OHS)

Occupational Health and Safety (OHS) is all about identifying and assessing risk in your work environment and aiming to reduce or eliminate this. Whilst most employers undertake a detailed OHS assessment of their workplace, staff who telework often miss out on a formal review. However, many employers who have a telework policy and/or who have a significant portion of their workforce who undertake regular telework, will provide a formal OHS review of the relevant employees' home work space.

The best place to start when assessing your OHS readiness is with your employer's OHS representative. He/she will be able to outline the requirements of your home-based work area and may provide a checklist for you to work from.

A basic OHS checklist for teleworkers might include the following:

- Good ventilation
- Ample space to ensure comfort
- Easy access to required equipment
- Safe and tidy layout of office area (walkways and passages should be clear of electrical cables)
- Adequate lighting, heating, cooling
- Secure management of files / documents / equipment
- Manageable workload
- Adequate variation in your tasks (to avoid repetitive strain injuries)
- Suitable ergonomic furniture, i.e., desks and chairs should be adjustable to suit your comfort levels
- Position of work area, especially computer screens, should be devoid of glare or other hazardous conditions

As regulations differ according to which state/territory you live in, you will need to consult with your relevant government body governing the OHS regulations in your location. Check out the Telework Australia's OHS page which lists the relevant government departments in each Australian state/territory.

http://www.teleworkaustralia.net.au

Family support and coordination

Your family and household members are a integral component to achieving success in your telework endeavour. Every person you reside with or interact with regularly in your home needs to understand and respect the boundaries of your work space and schedule – and vice-versa, it's also important that your work plans take into consideration the needs of your family as well. It simply won't work otherwise.

When planning to start working from home, involve your partner and children (and other members of your household) as much as possible. Make them aware of your plans and needs to get their buy-in. This will most certainly provide the support you need to be an effective teleworker.

Useful References

- www.teleworkaustralia.net.au

- www.whirlpool.net.au

Chapter 11

Starting a Home-Based Business

Around one third of small businesses in Australia are home-based.

Source: www.business.vic.gov.au

Running your own business can provide a great deal of flexibility. As your own boss you make the decisions about what, when, where and how you work. You can also make the choice to start off small, operating your business on a part-time basis and then expanding when you are ready and willing.

Starting off from home provides all the benefits of being a home-based worker which has been described in detail throughout this book. For a business owner, operating from home also means that broader benefits and financial savings are possible through:

- reduced barriers to entry
- reduced operating costs
- reduced startup costs
- lower overheads than bricks and mortar
- sharing some utilities or services with household use, therefore reducing running costs or setup fees

- being able to legitimately claim applicable tax deductions via the tax system

> **Around 18% of working mothers are self-employed or contractors. Over one third of these became self-employed to meet the demands of their caring responsibilities.**
>
> Source: *Australian Institute of Family Studies, 2005.*

For many mums the decision to re-enter the workforce via self employment, freelancing or contracting is largely driven by the need to secure flexibility around work to care for their children. It also means that they don't have to go through many of the hurdles experienced by mums attempting to re-enter the workforce as an employee, such as negotiating work hours, flexible working arrangements, etc.

A basic ingredient for starting a successful business is sound research, together with an objective perspective. Quite often what will happen is that we fall in love with the idea of our own business and don't foresee the limitations and pitfalls, making us unprepared for the reality of it all.

As a mum you know what your limitations are in terms of time, commitment, availability, etc. Being clear about your business needs and how you can manage these requirements, within your scope as a mum, must be assessed realistically.

What you put into your business will affect what you get out of it; therefore you need to set your expectations on solid ground. Whilst not impossible, it's generally unrealistic to start a business on a shoestring budget, devote only a couple of hours' of work each week and expect huge returns.

> ### Life Story
>
> Cathryn was a primary school teacher but left her job soon after returning from maternity leave. She tried returning to work on a casual basis when her first child was one, but living in a NSW country town made it difficult for her to secure suitable child care. School teaching was not a job she could do from home, which is what her heart desired, so she quit her job.
>
> Whilst pregnant to her second child Cathryn decided to start her own online business. Having experienced difficulty in finding good quality and variety in baby clothing and accessories she decided to source these from the city and promote them to her townsfolk and neighbouring towns. She made them available through her online store and promoted it via word of mouth and advertising in regional newspapers.

What type of business can I run from home?

There are many businesses that you can operate from home that are also suitable for mums with caring responsibilities. Chapter 6 provides a good starting point with regards to the best and worst jobs and industries for telework. This should serve as a guide to deciding on what business would be suitable to undertake from home.

Some businesses cannot be operated from home, e.g., mechanical repairs and major manufacturing requiring industrial machinery. Check with your local council before deciding to proceed so that you have peace of mind knowing that your business idea at least complies with your council's regulations.

Have a plan

A business plan is essentially your roadmap to success. This should be thoroughly researched and documented, and revised when needed. It serves to keep you focused on your goals and values, without veering off on a trifle tangent. A known cause of significant business troubles is linked with the absence of a business plan.

Online businesses

Online businesses offer mums the flexibility to run their business from home – without huge overheads of bricks and mortar – yet still appear as professional as any other business. As orders come through 24 x 7, response times are generally acceptable within several hours and do not necessarily need to be instant. However, technology provides innovative methods to support business processes. There are now many automated systems to help you generate, manage and process sales, leads and enquiries, without the need for immediate human interaction.

Build a website

You don't need to operate an online business to have a website. In fact, if you don't have a website these days, your business could very well run the risk of being outrun by your competitors!

Aside from making it easier to find your business, having an online presence offers customers much sought after information that clients like to source prior to engaging a new supplier, contractor or business partner.

There has been a huge shift towards online advertising and many businesses and individuals utilise the web to source information and also to communicate and collaborate with others online. Developing a website is not necessarily an expensive outlay either. There are now many website builders which provide the opportunity to create your own website for free! Whilst some of these are not as swish as having your site commissioned by a professional web designer, they can certainly help you add value and a new dimension to your business. You can always upgrade your site with these providers or opt for a new one once you decide to take your online presence to the next level.

Sites offering free 'build-your-own website' opportunities sometimes come with a 'catch'. Some providers offer free websites when you display their advertising, others offer a free limited trial period only. So, look into what the terms and conditions are before investing your time in setting one of these sites up. Check out some of the following:

- www.webs.com
- www.homestead.com
- wordpress.org

Working to schedule

Establishing what your business needs to function smoothly on a day to day basis is essential for busy mums. Mapping out your day, week, month and year in advance is a great way to see what your schedule holds ahead, allowing you to smooth out any conflicting tasks or timeframes. It also helps you prepare your daily routine, thereby increasing your productivity by optimising your time. A great way to do this is to allocate priority levels for each task that needs to be done. Example:

A = Top priority, essential tasks
B = Should do tasks
C = Nice to do tasks

Date: Monday 8th October

Priority	Task
A	Respond to client enquiries
A	Finish client order
B	Prepare client invoice
B	Prepare client quotation
C	Complete BAS statement

Once you have your priority levels assigned, work out the order in which you need to complete each task. You can do so by ordering the tasks within each priority with numbers. Example:

Date: Monday 8th October

Priority	Task
A1	Finish client order
A2	Respond to client enquiries
B1	Prepare client quotation
B2	Prepare client invoice
C1	Complete BAS statement

www.teleworkingmum.com.au

Outsourcing

Outsourcing some of your non-core business tasks is a great way to free up your time when you need it, to either attend to your duties as a mum or to concentrate on your key business offering (i.e., your products or services). It's also a great way to present yourself as a professional business without having to outlay much money. When starting off small, it's also more cost effective than hiring staff.

There are many services you can outsource for your business. Some common support services include:

- Reception / telephone answering
- Administration, data entry, bookkeeping
- Secretarial, faxing, typing, diary management
- Marketing, advertising, promotions
- Communications, writing, research
- Design, web design, graphic design

There are many other services you can outsource. What you choose to outsource will depend on your business requirements, your skills, your finances and your time. Also, why not think about outsourcing some of your home duties such as ironing, cleaning or laundry work? This will most certainly free up much of your time to devote to your new business.

Networking

Running a business can be quite daunting. There is so much that you need to know, learn and keep across, and if you are running your business solo the ability to find time to locate these resources and keep up to date adds a lot of pressure on small business leaders.

There are many online and local resources available to assist with keeping abreast of key business issues as well as providing avenues for developing valuable contacts (and needless to say can provide the social interaction you often lack). Consider taking some time out to research relevant online networking organisations and either make contact or join ones that interest you. The beauty of keeping in contact this way is that you can choose how involved you become – whether it's simply following an organisation on Twitter to keep abreast of their news, or becoming an active member of their online or offline community. Following is a suggestion of some categories to search on via your preferred search engine:

- **Online support groups**
- **Networking groups**
- **Women's business groups**
- **Local business incubators (see local councils)**

Pricing

Be careful when pricing your products or services to ensure that you don't sell yourself short. Know what you, your products or services are worth by doing some market research. If you are able to offer competitive pricing, that's great, as long as you factor in all your costs. As a home-based business you don't have the huge bricks and mortar overheads of retail or office space to cover, so pricing can be more flexible. However, don't offer prices that are too low, as you may run the risk of associating your business brand with inferior products or services. Consumers often associate quality with price in the middle to high end of the market. Instead, use opening specials or seasonal promotions to discount your products/services as one offs to attract new clients. However, if you're intentionally targeting the lower end of the market, offer as many bargains as you can. Your customers will love it!

Be confident

Nobody wants to do business with someone who lacks confidence about themselves, their business, their products or services. Learn to love your business by immersing yourself in knowledge about what you are offering to appreciate its value to the fullest. Educate yourself to become a specialist within your field – this will give your confidence a boost which will undoubtedly shine through when dealing with your customers and suppliers as well.

Financing your business

Financing a startup can be tricky for some people, although there have been many successful businesses which were built on a shoestring budget!

Credit cards are a viable option for the small business owner and are easier to obtain than business loans. It is important, however, to keep strictly to your 30 day terms to pay back your balance, otherwise interest charges and fees could blow out your budget and eat into your profit margins.

Follow up your debtors

Debtors are people or businesses who owe you money. As a small business operator it is often necessary to provide flexible trading terms to attract more customers to your business. These days it is fairly common to offer 30 day accounts. Some businesses also offer shorter trading terms such as 7 days or 14 days to bring in the cashflow more regularly.

What happens a lot in the business world is that businesses take the liberty to extend their payments so that their own cashflow is less affected. It is quite common nowadays for businesses to extend a 30 day cycle to 60 days or beyond. In a tough economic climate this can be crippling for your business – particularly if your customer base is small.

Small business operators often feel embarrassed to contact their clients about their unpaid accounts; they don't want to ruin the rapport they have worked hard to establish. The consequences, however, in holding up your cash flow is too great. You need to work out simple yet effective strategies to deal with your customer accounts.

Manage your credit cards

Many small businesses use their credit cards to purchase stock and / or supplies for their business. Whilst this is a viable means of credit, the repayments on cards should be managed wisely. As some credit cards charge 16% interest per annum, other ones are as high 25% per annum. Therefore this interest is added to your stock prices, so your profit margins are reduced. As with the need for cash flow and asking your customers to pay on time, you also need to manage these kinds of bills with more caution so as not to blow out your budget without realising it.

Get good help

Many of us are reluctant to ask for, or accept, help. Well, imagine what your life would be like if you actually accepted a helping hand once in a while. When good help is there, use it.

However, on the flip side, if someone who is offering help is turning out to be more of an impediment than a benefit, you need to take control and relieve them of their duties. Be diplomatic but firm about it.

Organisation

Running a business can demand loads of time. As a mum your time is already in short supply with your family taking up a good chunk of it. One of the most critical success factors in running a business when you're a mum is organisation. So, plan ahead and account for every minute of the day so that you run to a tight schedule to minimise underutilised time. Of course things don't always go as planned when kids are involved; however, build an element of flexibility into your routine so that things don't fall into a shambles when one task gets missed. But that's one reason why mums make such great business owners: they're usually prepared with a backup plan!

Take it seriously

A home based business is a serious business. You need to go through the process of setting it up correctly, ensuring your financial and legal obligations are met. There are various local, state and federal laws and regulations that businesses in Australia are bound by. The best place to start is the Australian government's portal on business which provides a step by step plan to establish, register and setup your business. Go to **www.business.gov.au**. Here you will find some very useful information as well as links to all state government bodies throughout Australia. Another crucial step is to call your local council or log on to their website to ensure you comply with their requirements as well.

Home business tips

- Build customer relationships. Spend time to get to know your customers then work with them to understand what they really want. Then work hard at delivering to meet or exceed their expectations.
- Always follow up on enquiries - never assume touching base is a waste of time.

- Treat cancellations with courtesy and these customers are more likely to come back.
- Touch base with customers after you have filled their orders. Feedback is an essential element to developing a successful business and you may find that they are ready to place yet another order! Also, new customers cost more to establish and service, so always focus on developing your existing customer base first.
- Shop around for the best offer from suppliers. Developing good relationships with your suppliers places you in a better position to negotiate better terms and prices with them.
- Streamline your processes to cut unnecessary time and costs.
- Find your niche and your competitive advantage and use it to sell your business.
- Don't fret the small stuff! Time is precious, so stop wasting time on things that don't make much difference to your customers or your business.
- Outsource where possible to allow you to focus on critical business tasks and core functions.
- Work on your wellbeing. The business will fail if you're run down, stressed or ill. It is essential you allow time for yourself.
- Start off small – there's no reason why you can't run your business on a part-time basis. Some online businesses are so automated and virtual there's no need to work set hours. You can allocate your work time when it suits you.
- Contingency planning: plan ahead to deal with life's stumbling blocks before they happen. Develop a back-up plan if you are forced to temporarily withdraw from the business.

Useful References

- www.business.gov.au

Chapter 12

Teleworking Mum's Timeline

Each stage of a child's development will pose different challenges for the teleworking mum. There are distinctive temperaments, needs and inclinations for children of similar age groups, so it's helpful to know what some of these are to consider any adjustments to your work style or routine, before the next phase begins.

I remember the predicament with my first child: as soon as I was beginning to down pat my work schedule in line with his routine, he developed new behaviours and needs which changed the way I was able to work. Sleep patterns is a good example. As a baby my son would always wake up around 6:30am and then have a two hour nap from 9-11am. I would schedule my work around this time which generally tended to be free of distractions. As he approached twelve months, his night nap was extended and day time naps were shortened. So, my schedule was reshuffled. Then, when he entered the terrible twos, boy was I in for some major re-adjusting!

This chapter captures some of the key characteristics of each major age group for children, from the perspective of a mum who is juggling both family and work responsibilities.

Of course each child is different; however, there are some common patterns of behaviour which can be generally applied to each main phase of a child's development. Knowing what some of these are in advance is useful in preparing a successful teleworking journey.

Age Group: 0-12 months

Opportunities

The baby stage is one of the best times to embark on your teleworking journey, whether it is as an employee or via your own business. Babies sleep often and if you don't have other children you can usually find a routine to devote to your work for one or two hours at a time. It's also incredibly rewarding to be at home during this time to experience and bond with your new baby to the fullest.

Issues

This can be one of the most emotionally and physically trying times for mothers. Some babies can be temperamental and some don't seem to sleep at all.

Taking on too much work at this stage will defeat the purpose of working from home: you may risk missing out on the enormous rewards that bonding with your baby may bring. It's also imperative that you take time out for yourself to heal and recover from any physical and emotional stress you may have experienced with your pregnancy and / or labour.

Success Factors

I started working from home when my first child was five months old. At this point I was in the midst of a wellbeing crisis: lack of sleep, aches and pains, fatigue, etc. I started working two hours from home, five days a week. I recall noticing a marked improvement in my outlook on life soon after I started working again. The hours I took on were flexible to a certain degree and very manageable within the demands of my day. This took the pressure off feeling overwhelmed by not biting off more than I could chew. I enjoyed the work I was doing which gave me a sense of achievement and the autonomy of the role gave me the freedom to put my stamp on it and develop it as I went along.

Flexibility and starting off small are the key success factors for mums starting off on their work at home journey during this stage of your child's life.

Age Group: 1 - 3 years

Opportunities

Some mothers find that this is the best time for routines, especially day-time naps. It therefore becomes easier to judge when to schedule your work hours and how many hours are manageable.

Issues

This age group encompasses the terrible two's of toddlerhood. Left unsupervised, toddlers are capable of creating mayhem – not to mention the high risk of accidents. This is also possibly the noisiest age group: if you're toddler isn't throwing a tantrum, most likely he will be playing with a noisy toy with all the bells and whistles! And what's the bet that both will occur when you're on the phone to a client!

Success Factors

As in the earlier age group, this group of children requires extensive supervision and therefore it is not suitable to be undertaking extended hours of work. Try scheduling shorter periods of work; make phone calls while your child is asleep or while he is being supervised by another adult, or in childcare. If you need to work whilst your toddler is awake try setting up an activity table near your desk so that you can supervise him. He may be less likely to play up if he acknowledges your presence, and of course will appreciate your company.

Age Group: 3 - 5 years

Opportunities

During this time your child may commence kindergarten. Although sessions times are usually short (typically 2-5 hours across two to three days per week), it still provides some free time for mums. Use these hours to 'power-work', i.e., focus your undivided attention on your job to achieve high levels of productivity for great results.

Issues

The drawback of kindergarten is preparation and travel time. Many mums comment on the time it takes to get their children to kinder and then back home again, leaving less time in between for them to focus on work or other tasks.

Success Factors

Planning is the key to success for this stage. Plan your work ahead so that you know exactly what needs to be done during the time you set aside for your 'power-work' session, regardless of how small the time frame is. Be well prepared and have any tools, equipment, information, files, etc., at your fingertips the minute you commence your power work session.

Age Group: 5 – 11 years

Opportunities

Most children usually commence school around the age of five. For teleworking mums, this provides you with more day time to devote to your work or business. This may be an ideal time to start your business or ramp it up if you started off small whilst your child was in his pre-school years.

Your child matures considerably during this time so is able to understand the need for you to work and may even appreciate getting involved in some way. Try to gauge if they are interested and if so find suitable tasks that they can regularly do, e.g., filing or mailing. Perhaps if you allow your child some pocket money for school then they can earn it with some light duties to assist you in your work or business.

Issues

As your child's social sphere expands there is more demand on parents to get involved, especially as the dedicated driver! Therefore it's best to stick to your work routine during school hours and focus on your children and home life outside these hours.

Also, with the increased social exposure, children are more susceptible to catching colds and lurgies! So it's important to keep a flexible back-up plan in place for your work as you may need to plan for days that your child is sick at home.

Success Factors

Keep yourself organised and confine your work routine to school hours. Focus fully on your family and personal issues outside of this time. However, develop a plan ahead of time for school holidays. Either reduce your workload during these weeks or take some time off to spend quality time with your child.

Age Group: 12 + years

Opportunities

During this stage your child tends to enter secondary school. As your child gets older they can do more for themselves and parents should encourage them to take on some household responsibilities – within reason.

Issues

This is a very busy time for families and a very crucial period whereby performance at school lays the foundation for your child's future. It's also a very emotionally demanding time – for both children and parents. Children become adolescents and start dealing with huge changes in their lives. Your guidance and involvement as a parent is very critical during this period.

Success Factors

Your involvement as a parent during this time forges your relationship with your child as they prepare to enter adulthood. Devote ample time outside of school hours to support your children during this eventful stage of their lives.

As they gear towards adulthood you can benefit by freeing up some of your time by enlisting their help around the house for suitable household chores or errands.

Life Story

I laughed hysterically as I put the book down to wipe my tears and contain myself, in fear of waking up my children who were asleep in the next room. I was reading an article titled *'How I Became an Author in the Back of My Minivan'* in the latest Chicken Soup for the Soul series.[12]

The author, Wendy Walker, recounts how as a stay-at-home mum, she wrote her book on her laptop in the back seat of her minivan - in between kinder drop off and pick up times - in attempt to creatively reclaim precious time to devote to her writing.

As a busy stay-at-home mum, your day is filled with an endless string of things to do. Housework, cooking, washing, taxi duties, shopping, nappy changes, the list goes on. How do you manage to fit in work or the personal pleasures that we crave so much?

Wendy Walker's micro-managing antics are both radical and resourceful; yet, she successfully manages, within her busy schedule as a mum, to find time for her love of writing. Yes, it's funny - even absurd - yet at the same time, it's also inspiring. With so much to do, within so little time, it's easy to feel defeated and just give up; but if you really put your heart and mind to it, you'd be surprised at what you can achieve.

---

[12] Canfield, J., Hansen, M, V., Walker, W., *Power Moms, Chicken Soup for the Soul, 2009.*

www.teleworkingmum.com.au

Chapter 13

Your Journey Begins

Earning an income in conjunction with your non paid labour and parenting responsibilities can be challenging to say the least. Whilst you strive to provide financially, emotionally and practically, it's easy to get caught in a cycle of chaos, without stopping to question its worth or efficacy. Deep down you long for a better way to manage your work/life fit - hopefully this book has shed some positive light on your plea.

There comes a time when, as a working mum, you need to accept that you can't be everything to everyone all the time. Realistic limitations and expectations need to be managed, and it all starts with you. What you believe is okay is what others around you will pick up on your invisible radar. You need to affirm: 'this is where I draw the line', or 'this is all I can manage at the moment'. It's ok to call for help, delegate or outsource tasks that simply don't fit within your capacity threshold. Yes, we all have our limits, and that's ok.

Whether this is relevant to home or work, you need to communicate with the people around you so that you don't get to the point where you feel you're drowning. Time is a significant issue for working women, with recent studies indicating that around 60% of working women feel rushed or pressed for time[13]. There still remains the expectation for women to also bear the brunt of a considerable part of the non-paid labour required to sustain a household, as well as upholding their primary care responsibilities for children in addition to their paid labour efforts.

As you begin to prepare yourself and your family for your teleworking journey, it's worthwhile to take some time to reflect on yourself as an individual and consider your own needs, desires and aspirations. As a mum no doubt you're always quick to action the needs and demands of your family, yet somehow, in midst of all the 'to do's' and 'have to's' we tend to let our own needs drift by the wayside.

We hear or read about the conflicts experienced by many mums returning to the workforce, and particularly of their 'mother guilt'. Somehow leaving your child in someone else's care in order to attend your employment incites much emotional trepidation for many mums. I think the 'mother guilt' concept is often used incorrectly to refer to many different situations, some of which are not necessarily driven by guilt, but rather, a mindful preference to be with your child. There's nothing wrong with wanting to be with your child; yet, when that desire is not fulfilled due to lack of a suitable work/life options, we naturally feel saddened by our circumstances. That's one reason why flexibility in the workplace is in such high demand, particularly

---

[13] Pocock et al, *AWALI*, 2009.

telework arrangements, as it affords us the choice to be with our children more — a pure element of life that should be encouraged, not restricted

For these and other reasons, most women experience a sizeable shift in the way they re-engage in the workforce once they become mothers. Some change careers, or employers, or work hours. Others abandon the workforce by choice or by compulsion.

This book is essentially a self-help guide, assisting you to strengthen your knowledge and broaden your work-choice perspective. As it stands, whilst there has been recent legislation in Australia supporting workplace flexibility, it is largely up to you to equip yourself with the information and understanding required to re-engage or maintain your position in the workforce whilst also managing your duties as a mum. I would like to see the government and employers accepting some of this liability by offering a long term commitment to programs and strategies for mums. Such programs will improve the quality of life for working mums, who are single-handedly dealing with the difficulties resulting from the need to fulfill the double role of primary carer and income earner (and not to mention the often taken-for-granted role of homemaker).

Whilst not a program or strategy per se, teleworking offers an alternative route for returning to work or maintaining your employment when you're a mum. It bypasses many of the struggles and barriers, making workforce participation more achievable for some mums.

Teleworking offers many benefits for working parents, two key ones being that of saving time and money. Teleworking also holds some organic perks which add to its appeal (such as environmental benefits, tax benefits and community benefits). The beauty of teleworking and other flexible working arrangements is that it can be deployed when you need it the most, and relinquished when no longer mutually suitable for you and your employer. Allowing provision for a review period in your telework or flexible working arrangement is one of the most critical aspects to formalising your agreement. What works for you now may not be what serves you best when your child starts school, or when other aspects of your life change.

With the increase in Australia's ageing population, more people are remaining in the workforce longer. Mature workers are looking to wind down their careers and are seeking more flexibility – particularly telework – to maintain their quality of life. Therefore, whilst you might start teleworking now to juggle your work with family, you might also look to telework at the latter end of your career. And somewhere in between, there might also come a time when you experience a change in caring responsibilities (for example, ill or elderly family member). In these circumstances, teleworking also offers substantial benefits.

This book has taken me two and a half years to create. Most of the writing has been done in the evenings whilst my family was sleeping. By comparison, if I did not assume the role of primary carer for my children, I would have completed this book in less than eight months. However, I would have also missed out on irreplaceable moments I shared with my children. I would have also missed out on a large part of the maternal role I longed to fulfill. This is the choice I made, the decision which pleased my family and I the most, which is really the whole crux of this book.

This book was written to encourage and empower mums to embrace a better lifestyle by equipping them with the knowledge and confidence to explore better work choices. Mum or career woman? It doesn't have to be strictly one or the other. There really can be a happy medium between work and family life and you have the right to choose what is best for you.

www.teleworkingmum.com.au

Index

Business 115, 171-183
Childcare 64-72
Cottage industry 102, 116
Employer
   tips 144-145
   objections (dealing with) 131-135
Equipment 129, 139
Insurance 46, 51-52, 139, 159
Flexibility 20
   new laws 84-89
   types of 89-93
Technology 159-163
Financial benefits 11-12, 39-42
Freelancing 114-115
Tax benefits 42-54
Workforce
   re-entry 14, 55-64, 72-81
   women in 17-20

Legal
   council regulations 165-167
   occupational health & safety 167-168
Online Marketplaces 116
Scams 118-120
Social networking 111
Telework
   agreement 137-143
   benefits 25-37
   best & worst industries 97-99
   best & worst jobs 99-103
   definition 21
   mum's timeline 185-192
   proposal 122-131
   obstacles 34-37
   opportunities 107-117
Workplaces
   family friendly 16-17, 147-152

References

1. Australian Bureau of Statistics. *Australian Social Trends*, 2008.
2. Australia Bureau of Statistics. *Labour Force, Australia*, 2009.
3. Australia Bureau of Statistics. *Locations of Work*, 2008.
4. Australian Bureau of Statistics. *Census of Population and Housing: Selected Social and Housing Characteristics*, 2006.
5. Australian Institute of Family Studies. *Parents who don't use childcare: who provides the care in working families with infants?* 2009.
6. Australian Institute of Family Studies. *Growing up in Australia Study*, 2008.
7. Canfield J, Hansen M, Walker W. *Power Moms: Chicken Soup for the Soul*, 2009.
8. Equal Opportunity for Women in the Workplace Agency (EOWA). *Generation F*, 2008.
9. Human Rights Equal Opportunity Commission. *Striking the balance : women, men, work and family discussion paper*, 2005.
10. Pocock B, Skinner N, Ichii R. *Australian Work and Life Index: Work, Life and Workplace Flexibility*, University of South Australia, 2009.
11. Toshiba. *Mobility and Mistruts*, 2004,
12. www.ato.gov.au
13. www.breastfeedingfriendly.com.au
14. www.deewr.gov.au
15. www.dhcs.act.gov.au
16. www.eowa.gov.au
17. www.earlychildhoodaustralia.org.au
18. www.fairwork.gov.au
19. www.parentsreturningtowork.com.au
20. www.teleworkaustralia.com.au
21. www.teleworkingmum.com.au
22. ways2work.business.vic.gov.au

About the Author

Maria Montesano is a Melbourne based researcher with almost two decades of experience. Throughout her career Maria has undertaken research and related work for various corporate and academic organisations including Deakin University, The University of Melbourne and Computer Sciences Corporation.

Since becoming a mum in 2005, Maria has freelanced her services through her own home-based business, Red Bullet Research and Communications.

www.ingramcontent.com/pod-product-compliance
Lightning Source LLC
Chambersburg PA
CBHW020948230426
43666CB00005B/217